If Looks Could Kill

The Aubrey Gold Story

By Kelli Roberts

Copyright

No part of this book may be reproduced, reverse-engineered, transmitted in any form or by any means, graphic, electronic, or mechanical, including photocopy, recording, taping, or by any information storage or retrieval system, without the permission in writing from the publisher except in the case of brief quotation embodied in critical articles and reviews. Please respect the hard work of the author and do not post or share this work.

This book explores the real crimes committed by real people. All the information presented here, apart from my own observations, has been sourced from official records or through interviews with individuals directly connected to the lives of those mentioned.

In "If Looks Could Kill: The Aubrey Gold Story," Kelli Roberts offers an unflinching look at the rise and downfall of Lauren Wambles, known by her stage name Aubrey Gold. This gripping true crime book dives deep into the world of a young woman who dreamed of stardom but found herself serving a 10-year prison sentence for her involvement in the murder of Raul Ambriz Guillen.

Kelli Roberts, a seasoned expert in the adult industry with nearly thirty years of experience, provides a unique insider perspective. Her narrative not only explores Aubrey's tumultuous career but also illuminates the often misunderstood aspects of the adult film industry.

From the small town of Dothan, Alabama to the chaotic frenzy of Las Vegas, Aubrey's journey was fraught with challenges. Driven by aspirations and besieged by hardships, her life was a rollercoaster of highs and devastating lows. This book delves into her transition from an adult film star to a convicted criminal, examining the intricate web of her decisions, relationships, and the systemic failures that shaped her tragic path.

Kelli Roberts challenges the sensationalized versions of Aubrey's story portrayed in media and true crime documentaries, which often link her criminal actions simplistically to her adult film career. "If Looks Could Kill" seeks to provide a comprehensive and nuanced view of Aubrey's life, advocating for a deeper understanding of her as more than just a headline.

Join Kelli as she uncovers the real story behind Aubrey Gold's public persona, offering insights into the human complexity behind the crimes and providing a thoughtful critique of the societal judgments that influence public perception.

This book is a must-read for fans of true crime and those interested in the dynamics of the adult industry, offering a poignant exploration of the delicate interplay between individual choices and societal forces.

Table of Contents

The Crime and the Witness

The phone lit the room before I understood why I was awake. It was still dark, the hour when every sound feels amplified and every piece of bad news arrives with an unreal quality. I reached toward the glow on my nightstand and saw a headline about a former adult film performer arrested in connection with a murder in Florida.

Then I saw the photograph. Lauren Wambles. But I knew her as *Aubrey Gold*.

For a moment, the two names seemed to belong to different people. Lauren was the young woman from Dothan, Alabama, who had tried to build a life far beyond the reach of her childhood. Aubrey was the name she carried into the adult industry, bright and polished, chosen to suggest value, success, and transformation.

The woman in the mugshot looked like neither of them. Her face was familiar, but the expression wasn't. The lively young performer I remembered seemed gone. Her eyes looked emptied out by exhaustion, fear, drugs, or some combination of all three. The photograph carried none of the glamour once associated with her stage name. There were no lights, no makeup chair, no camera crew waiting for her to smile.

There was only the flat illumination of a booking room. I read the headline again.

A man named Raul Ambriz Guillen was dead. Aubrey had been arrested in connection with his murder.

While I wouldn't say we were "close" or even friends, I had spoken with her when she found herself trapped in a professional relationship, she no longer wanted and couldn't easily escape. Now she was attached to a crime so violent that it seemed to erase every version of her that had existed before it.

That's what a murder headline does. It compresses a human life into a few words. Former porn star. Murder. Arrest. Prison. The details came later.

On July 4, 2020, while fireworks cracked across the rural Florida sky, Raul was shot in the back of the head at a house in Holmes County. According to the prosecution's case and Aubrey's later statements, she helped bring him to the location under the pretense of a holiday gathering. Her boyfriend, William Shane Parker, was accused of carrying out the killing. Jeremie "JP" Peters was tied to the debt and criminal network surrounding the crime.

Raul's body was buried in a shallow grave. It remained hidden until August 25, 2020.

By the time the case moved through the courts, one man had been sentenced to life without parole, another received twenty years, and Lauren Wambles had received a ten-year prison sentence after cooperating with the state. Those facts are simple enough to summarize. Understanding them is far more difficult.

A man was lured to his death. A young woman I once knew helped create the circumstances that made it possible.

Nothing in this book changes that. Context isn't absolution. Trauma isn't innocence. Addiction doesn't erase moral responsibility. Exploitation doesn't excuse participation in violence.

Raul died because several people made choices that placed his life beneath their fear, jealousy, loyalty, debt, and self-preservation. His family continues to live with an absence no prison sentence can repair.

That must remain at the center of this story. True crime often pulls attention away from the person who died. The victim becomes a plot point while the accused becomes the spectacle. In Aubrey's case, the adult industry connection made that imbalance almost inevitable. A former adult performer tied to a murder was irresistible to documentary producers, podcasters, and news outlets.

The story came prepackaged with scandal. It only needed a title.

Within months, the familiar narrative began to form. Aubrey had entered pornography. Pornography had corrupted her. Her life had spiraled downward until murder became the natural conclusion.

It was dramatic. It was marketable and it was also far too simple.

I've worked in the adult industry for nearly thirty years. I entered the business during an era of VHS tapes, print advertisements, mail-order catalogs, and websites that loaded one image at a time. I watched the industry move through DVDs, streaming platforms, social media, clip stores, subscription pages, and performer-owned businesses.

I have worked behind the scenes as a producer, webmaster, consultant, and advocate. I have watched performers arrive with carefully built plans and others arrive with little more than hope. Some treated the work as a temporary job. Some built long careers. Some saved money, bought homes, started businesses, raised families, or moved into entirely different professions.

Others struggled. I have watched young women sign contracts they didn't understand. I have watched agents use fear and isolation to maintain control. I have seen performers arrive on set already carrying addiction, family trauma, financial instability, and emotional wounds that the industry neither created nor knew how to address.

I have also seen people within the business step forward to help. They drove performers to treatment. They confronted abusive producers. They helped newcomers understand testing, consent, contracts, taxes, and boundaries. They offered couches, legal referrals, food, money, and quiet companionship when the cameras were gone.

The adult industry contains both care and exploitation because human beings contain both. It isn't a single machine that transforms everyone who enters it. It is a collection of people, companies, working conditions, power structures, opportunities, and failures. Some environments are professional. Others are predatory. Many exist somewhere between those extremes.

Aubrey entered that world young, ambitious, and emotionally vulnerable. That vulnerability didn't make her incapable of choice.

It made the consequences of her choices more complicated. My direct involvement in her life began through advocacy work. A mutual contact asked whether I could help her with a troubling agency situation. Aubrey wanted to leave The VIP Connect, which was operated by former performer Shy Love. She believed the arrangement was hurting her career, but she had been told she would need to pay thousands of dollars to get out.

Blacklisting frightened her. That fear matters in an industry built heavily on relationships and reputation. A performer can be legally free to walk away and still believe that doing so will cost her every future booking. One phone call from a powerful person can close doors that no court order can reopen quickly enough to pay next month's rent.

When I spoke with Aubrey, I didn't see a future criminal. I saw a young woman overwhelmed by a contract, money problems, professional isolation, and fear.

She was bright in some moments and deeply uncertain in others. She could be warm, funny, and charming. She could also be reckless, difficult, evasive, and increasingly dependent on alcohol.

She contained contradictions. That doesn't make her unusual.

It makes her human. What troubles me about the public retellings of her life is how quickly those contradictions disappear. The charming young woman is replaced by the manipulator. The frightened performer is replaced by the predator. Or the reverse happens, and she's stripped of responsibility entirely, portrayed as a helpless victim carried through every decision by stronger people.

Neither portrait is complete. Aubrey was vulnerable without being powerless, influenced without losing all agency, and harmed by others before helping cause terrible harm herself. Those truths occupy the same life.

That's the tension at the heart of this book. I'm writing as both an industry insider and someone who crossed paths with Aubrey before the murder made her name recognizable outside the adult industry. That position gives me access to parts of her story that other accounts have misunderstood or ignored.

It also creates a responsibility to question my own assumptions. Have I been too inclined to view her through the lens of exploitation because I have spent so many years advocating for performers?

Have others been too eager to view her as calculating because they are uncomfortable granting complexity to a woman involved in a brutal crime? Can both perspectives contain pieces of the truth?

These questions don't have easy answers. The available record offers facts, testimony, court documents, police interviews, professional opinions, and memories from people who knew her. It doesn't offer perfect access to her motives. Memory is unreliable. Self-preservation reshapes stories. Trauma distorts sequence and perception. Witnesses can be sincere and still be wrong.

Even confessions can contain strategy. William Shane Parker later made statements suggesting that he took responsibility because Lauren couldn't handle prison. His words raise an unresolved question about who physically carried out every act that night.

But that uncertainty can become its own distraction. Raul was lured to the house. He was killed. His body was concealed. Aubrey was there, participated in the events surrounding his death, and failed to report what happened. Whether she pulled the trigger or stood nearby doesn't erase her moral responsibility.

The legal system assigned different levels of punishment to each person involved. Shane received life without parole. JP received twenty years. Aubrey received ten. Does that represent justice? Perhaps in a legal sense. But what is justice when the dead can't return?

What does rehabilitation mean for someone who helped take another person's future? Can prison produce accountability, insight, and change, or does it merely contain damaged people until the state decides they have been punished long enough?

These questions extend beyond Aubrey. They reach into how we treat addiction, trauma, coercive relationships, economic desperation, and people leaving stigmatized professions. They challenge the belief that punishment alone can repair what neglect, violence, and poor choices have broken.

The criminal justice system is often asked to solve problems long after prevention has failed. By the time a judge sees a defendant, years of instability, addiction, abuse, missed intervention, and moral compromise may already have narrowed that person's life.

That doesn't mean the defendant should be excused. It means the courtroom is usually the final stop in a much longer story.

Aubrey's story began long before July 4, 2020. It began with Lauren Wambles, a child born to very young parents in Dothan, Alabama. It continued through family instability, school struggles, early dreams of escape, and a fascination with women who seemed powerful because people wanted them.

At eighteen, she left Alabama for Las Vegas and built a new identity from a stage name. Aubrey, borrowed from her mother's past.

Gold, chosen for the future she believed she deserved. She found work quickly. She built a fan base. She moved to Los Angeles. On the surface, she achieved the escape she had imagined.

But the economics beneath the image were harsher than the public understood. Performers were often paid flat fees, with no royalties. Testing, agent commissions, transportation, wardrobe, rent, and daily living expenses consumed much of what they earned. A performer could appear successful online while living one canceled booking away from financial crisis.

That pressure mattered. So did the people around her. Some tried to guide her. Some profited from her naivety. Some recognized her substance use but didn't know how to intervene. Some remembered her as joyful and affectionate. Others remembered hotel rooms damaged during drinking binges, drug use, emotional collapse, and a young woman who seemed increasingly unreachable.

When her career ended, the world she had built offered no clear path forward. She returned to Alabama without financial stability. Her grandmother, one of the few consistent figures in her life, was gone. The old hometown offered familiarity but little reinvention. Arrests followed. Drugs became more central. Her choices narrowed.

Then came Shane Parker. Older, controlling, and dangerous, he may have looked to Aubrey like protection at a moment when she felt she had none.

That relationship drew her into the orbit of JP Peters and Raul Guillen. The adult industry didn't murder Raul.

Aubrey's past work didn't pull a trigger. But the industry was part of her life, and its pressures, failures, and power imbalances can't be ignored simply because they don't provide a convenient cause.

The same is true of her childhood, her addiction, her relationships, and her financial desperation. None explains everything.

Together, they help us see the terrain across which she moved. This book will challenge several popular accounts of Aubrey's career and downfall. Some reports drastically understated her actual filmography. Others described royalties that adult performers generally don't receive. Many repeated industry claims without consulting people who understood how the business operated.

These may seem like small errors beside a murder. They aren't.

When basic facts are wrong, the larger interpretation becomes unstable. A false financial premise can create a false motive. An incomplete filmography can distort the length and scale of a career. A misunderstood agency relationship can hide coercion or exaggerate power.

Accuracy matters most when the subject is easy to sensationalize. I'm not asking readers to like Aubrey.

I'm not asking anyone to forgive her. I'm asking that we resist the comfort of a simple explanation.

People rarely move from childhood dreams to criminal tragedy in one dramatic leap. They arrive through accumulated choices, relationships, injuries, compromises, and failures. Some are personal. Some are systemic. Most are difficult to separate.

At several points in Aubrey's life, another outcome remained possible. Different interventions might have changed the road ahead: practical education before her first contract, financial guidance before the money disappeared, meaningful regulation of predatory agents, and treatment before alcohol and drugs overwhelmed her. A safer return home or an earlier break from Shane might also have opened another future. Raul, too, might have escaped if the money he requested had reached him in time.

The cruelty of these questions lies in the fact that none can change what happened. Raul is still dead.

His family still lives with that loss. Aubrey is still responsible for the choices that placed him in danger.

Yet the questions matter because another young person may already be moving through a similar landscape. Another performer may be signing a contract she doesn't understand. Another family may be mistaking addiction for moral failure. Another vulnerable person may be confusing control with protection.

Understanding the road doesn't undo the destination. It may help someone else avoid it.

This is the story of Lauren Wambles, who became Aubrey Gold and later became a prison inmate. It is also the story of Raul Ambriz Guillen, whose life should never be reduced to the crime that ended it.

It is a story about fame, shame, money, addiction, memory, exploitation, responsibility, and the limits of punishment. Above all, it is a story about how many warnings can appear before tragedy and how easily we recognize them only after someone is gone.

I wish I could say I saw the ending coming. I didn't. I saw a troubled young woman asking for help with an agent. Years later, I saw her face in a mugshot. Between those two images lies the story I'm trying to understand.

Sweet Home Alabama

The screen door slapped against its frame hard enough to rattle the glass. Lauren Wambles stood barefoot in the narrow hallway, listening as two adults argued in the next room. Their voices rose and fell beneath the hum of an overworked window air conditioner. Outside, cicadas screamed from the pine trees, their relentless chorus filling every pause.

She couldn't have explained what the argument was about. Money, perhaps. A missed promise. Someone who hadn't come home when they said they would. The details changed, but the sound remained the same.

A man's voice sharpened. A woman answered with equal force.

Then came the silence. That silence was always worse.

Lauren waited for a door to slam, an engine to start, or a voice to call her name. She had already learned that adults could disappear without warning. They could leave for an afternoon and return days later, or walk out carrying a bag and offer no explanation at all. Even when they stayed, they weren't always truly present.

So she remained in the hallway, small and watchful, trying to read the house through its noises. Children raised inside instability often become experts in weather no one else can see. They learn to recognize a storm through a tightened jaw, a cupboard closed too firmly, or the sudden quiet between two people who have run out of words. Lauren learned these lessons early. Long before she understood abandonment, addiction, shame, or resentment, she understood the need to pay attention.

Years later, people would describe her as impulsive. Reckless. Difficult. Manipulative. They would study her choices after a man was dead and ask what kind of woman could have helped bring him to his final moments.

But before she became a defendant, a performer, or a headline, Lauren was a child standing in a hot Alabama hallway, waiting to discover which version of home she would have that night. That's where her story begins. Not in Las Vegas. Not on a film set. Not beside a shallow grave in rural Florida. It begins in Dothan.

Dothan sits in the southeastern corner of Alabama, close enough to Florida and Georgia that leaving the state can feel easier than escaping the town itself. The city calls itself the Peanut Capital of the World, a title celebrated each autumn with carnival rides, livestock exhibitions, beauty pageants, fried food, and the National Peanut

Festival. The surrounding fields stretch beneath an enormous Southern sky, interrupted by gas stations, churches, low shopping plazas, and two-lane roads disappearing into pine.

From a distance, Dothan can look peaceful. Church steeples rise above neighborhoods of brick ranch houses and aging trailers. Friday-night football brings families into the stands beneath hard white stadium lights. Neighbors recognize one another in grocery store aisles. Children grow up with grandparents, cousins, teachers, and pastors all watching from overlapping circles.

That kind of community can offer belonging. It can also make privacy nearly impossible.

A family's troubles rarely remain inside the family. A mother's history, a father's arrest, a child's behavior at school, or a rumor whispered after Sunday service can become part of a person's public identity. Once a story attaches itself to someone, it can survive for years, passed from mouth to mouth until no one remembers where the truth ended and judgment began.

Lauren was born to parents who were barely more than children themselves. Her mother was sixteen. Her father was eighteen. They entered parenthood without the maturity, stability, or resources that raising a child demanded.

Their relationship was uncertain from the beginning. Whatever affection brought them together struggled beneath pressures neither was prepared to manage. Bills still arrived. Tempers flared. Promises were broken. The responsibilities of adulthood settled over two young people who hadn't finished becoming adults.

Lauren's mother had once worked as a stripper across the Florida state line. In another place, that job might have been treated as a private chapter in a young woman's life. In a conservative Southern community, it could become a permanent label.

People rarely asked what financial desperation had led her there. They didn't ask what choices she had been offered, or how few of them may have seemed possible. They saw the work and built a story around it.

The stigma followed her. Perhaps some of the judgment was spoken openly. Much of it likely arrived through pauses, expressions, exclusions, and invitations that never came. Shame doesn't always announce itself. Sometimes it sits beside you in a church pew. Sometimes it looks away in a grocery store. Sometimes it reaches the child of the person being judged.

Lauren inherited consequences for decisions she hadn't made. Her father was largely absent, appearing in fragments rather than providing a continuous presence. He moved through the edges of her childhood, there for periods and then gone again. His own problems made consistency difficult.

A child doesn't need legal language to understand that a parent is unreliable. She measures it in empty chairs, unanswered questions, and promises that become embarrassing to believe.

When he returned, Lauren may have wanted to trust him. Children often do.

They can forgive absences adults would find unforgivable because hope is one of the few forms of power available to them. A returning father can briefly restore the fantasy that this time will be different. Then he leaves again, and the child must decide whether to keep hoping or pretend she no longer cares.

That pattern can shape a person long after childhood ends. It can teach her that love arrives intensely and disappears suddenly. It can make instability feel familiar, even when it hurts. It can blur the difference between protection and control, attention and possession.

I have met many young women who entered the adult industry believing they were beginning entirely new lives. They changed their names, dyed their hair, moved across the country, and built public identities that appeared fearless. Yet the child they had been traveled with them.

Distance can change scenery. It doesn't erase the first lessons we learn about love.

By the time Lauren was seven, the instability surrounding her had become too serious to ignore. She was sent to live with her grandmother.

The move brought her into a home where meals arrived at regular times. Clothes were washed. Rules remained the same from one day to the next. The utilities stayed connected. The adults expected to be obeyed.

For a child raised around uncertainty, structure can feel like rescue. It can also feel like confinement.

Her grandmother's house offered safety, but safety came with expectations. There were limits on where Lauren could go, what she could wear, how she should speak, and what kind of girl she was expected to become. The disorder of her parents' home had been replaced by discipline. The change may have steadied her life, but it couldn't erase the restlessness already forming inside her.

A child can be grateful for shelter and still feel trapped by it. Both things can be true.

This is one of the difficulties in telling Lauren's story. People prefer simple categories. A home was either good or bad. A caregiver was either loving or cruel. A young woman was either exploited or fully in control. A defendant was either a victim or a villain.

Human lives rarely remain inside those borders. Her grandmother gave Lauren what her parents couldn't consistently provide. Yet structure alone couldn't meet every emotional need. Rules could organize her days, but they couldn't answer the question that may already have troubled her: Why hadn't her parents been able to keep her?

Lauren formed a particularly close bond with an aunt who was only eleven years older. The small age difference made the relationship feel less like a traditional aunt and niece arrangement and more like an alliance between sisters.

Her aunt occupied a middle ground between Lauren and the adults who controlled the house. She understood the rules but could laugh at them. She could offer sympathy without carrying the authority of a parent. Through her, Lauren caught glimpses of music, fashion, beauty, and a larger world beyond the limits of her grandmother's home.

That closeness mattered. When a child feels judged or misunderstood, one person who listens can become a lifeline. Yet even a loving relative can't always replace what has already been lost. Lauren still knew she was living in someone else's home because her own parents hadn't provided one she could remain in.

Her relatives were caring for her. She may not always have felt chosen.

Outside the house, Dothan continued teaching her what kinds of girls were accepted and what kinds weren't. The acceptable path was visible everywhere. Finish school. Stay out of trouble. Attend church. Find a respectable job or a dependable husband. Build a life close to the people who had watched you grow up.

Lauren seemed to want the opposite. She wanted to be seen, but not as the daughter of troubled parents.

She wanted attention, but not the suspicious attention of teachers, neighbors, or relatives waiting for her to fail. She wanted a future that belonged to her.

School became another place where authority and expectation pressed against her. She could be intelligent and perceptive when a subject interested her, but curiosity didn't translate into obedience. She struggled with attendance, discipline, and the growing conviction that what she was being taught had little connection to the life she intended to live.

Her appearance offered one of the few areas she could control. She shortened skirts after leaving home. Makeup appeared in school bathrooms. Hairstyles changed. Clothes became a language through which she could say what the adults around her didn't want to hear.

Look at me. I'm not who you think I am.

You don't get to decide who I become. To teachers and administrators, this may have looked like ordinary adolescent rebellion. To Lauren, each small act may have felt like proof that part of her still belonged to herself.

The trouble escalated. She skipped classes. She smoked cigarettes behind the school. She argued when she believed she was being singled out. Suspensions accumulated, creating a cycle in which every punishment made returning successfully more difficult.

Once a student becomes known as a problem, every mistake can seem to confirm the reputation already assigned to her. Was Lauren treated unfairly?

Perhaps at times. Was she also making choices that deepened the conflict? Almost certainly. Both can be true.

Her education slowly unraveled until she stopped attending. Dropping out narrowed her future, though it may have felt like liberation in the moment. School had become another building where adults measured her against standards she had stopped respecting. Leaving meant freedom from principals, attendance records, and the constant pressure to become someone she couldn't imagine being.

But freedom from one structure often creates dependence on another. Without a diploma, job prospects shrink. Without income, escape becomes harder. The person desperate to control her own life may become increasingly vulnerable to anyone promising a faster path out.

Lauren began searching for that path years before she was old enough to take it. At twelve, she saw adult content for the first time.

The fact has been repeated in accounts of her life because it appears to offer an easy explanation. A child watched pornography, became fascinated, entered the industry, and later fell into addiction and crime.

That version is neat. It is also dangerously incomplete.

Millions of people encounter adult material without building their identities around it. The screen alone didn't create Lauren's ambitions. What mattered was what she believed she saw there.

She didn't focus on the production crew, contracts, testing requirements, or the financial arrangement behind the images. She couldn't see how performers might be directed, edited, underpaid, pressured, bored, uncomfortable, or afraid. She saw a polished fantasy designed to conceal the labor that created it.

The women appeared wanted. They appeared confident.

Men watched them. Cameras centered them. Their beauty seemed to command attention rather than invite judgment. They looked, at least to a twelve-year-old girl, as though they controlled the room.

Lauren would later describe those women as powerful. I understand why that image might have taken hold of her.

A child who feels powerless doesn't always dream of safety. Sometimes she dreams of becoming impossible to ignore.

To Lauren, adult stardom may have represented more than sexuality. It offered a complete reversal of her place in the world. Instead of being the child people whispered about, she could become the woman everyone watched. Instead of being controlled, she could appear to control desire itself. Instead of waiting for adults to determine where she lived and how she behaved, she could earn money from the very qualities her community wanted hidden.

The fantasy offered a form of revenge. Not necessarily revenge against one person, but against an entire life that had made her feel small.

What she couldn't yet understand was the difference between being desired and being valued. That confusion isn't unique to the adult industry. It exists in advertising, modeling, music, entertainment, and social media. Young people are taught that visibility is power, then blamed when the attention they receive doesn't protect them.

Lauren began researching the lives she believed existed beyond Alabama. Las Vegas and Los Angeles appeared on computer screens as places of reinvention. Their names carried neon, palm trees, money, and possibility.

In Dothan, almost everyone knew where she came from. In a larger city, no one would.

The internet gave her a window into that imagined future. She could follow performers, study their photographs, and watch the public version of their lives unfold through posts designed to sell glamour. Hotel rooms looked expensive. Makeup was flawless. Compliments poured in from strangers.

What remained outside the frame? The unpaid bills. The testing fees. The agent's commission. The waiting. The rejection. The isolation of living among people who knew the persona but not the person.

Lauren saw the image. She didn't yet know the cost of producing it.

As she moved through adolescence, the distance between her and her family widened. Her mother's life may have represented everything Lauren feared becoming: trapped in the same region, burdened by old choices, working without ever feeling secure.

A daughter's determination not to become her mother can become its own kind of prison. Every similarity feels like danger. Every warning sounds like jealousy. Every attempt at guidance can be interpreted as an effort to drag her back toward a future she has already rejected.

Their relationship grew strained. Lauren wanted escape.

Her mother may have seen another form of danger approaching. But how could she warn her daughter away from a path that bore traces of her own history without Lauren hearing hypocrisy? How could a mother marked by community shame explain that the attention Lauren wanted might not become the freedom she imagined?

Perhaps the warnings came as anger. Perhaps Lauren answered with contempt.

Fear often disguises itself as both. By her later teens, Lauren's plan had become more concrete. She wasn't merely fantasizing about another life. She was preparing to leave.

She saved what money she could. She considered where she might go, who could help her, and what identity she would use when she arrived. Every private decision moved her closer to a future no one around her could approve.

The girl who had learned to listen for doors slamming was preparing to close one herself. I often return to this period of her life because it contains so many of the questions that later chapters can't resolve.

What might have happened if someone had taken her ambitions seriously without encouraging the fantasy? A mentor might have taken her ambitions seriously while explaining that one form of escape could create another form of captivity. School, counseling, or practical education might also have offered a path connected to the woman she hoped to become before people with less generous motives reached her.

These questions don't erase responsibility. They don't turn Lauren into an innocent carried helplessly from one event to the next. She made decisions. Some were reckless. Later, some became unforgivable.

Still, responsibility and vulnerability can exist in the same person. Lauren's life would eventually be examined backward from the murder of Raul Ambriz Guillen. Every childhood conflict would be treated as foreshadowing. Every act of rebellion would become evidence of what she was destined to do.

I don't believe lives work that neatly. A difficult childhood doesn't create a murderer.

Dropping out of school doesn't lead inevitably to prison. Entering the adult industry doesn't predict violent crime.

At each stage, other futures remained possible. That may be the most heartbreaking truth of all.

The roads leaving Dothan stretched in several directions. One could take Lauren toward Panama City, another toward Tallahassee, another north through Alabama. To a restless young woman, every highway may have seemed to promise transformation.

But she wasn't only trying to leave a town. She was trying to outrun a name, a family history, and the fear that everyone around her had already decided who she would become.

Soon, Lauren Wambles would choose a new name. She would borrow part of it from her mother and build the rest from the color of wealth, beauty, and victory.

Aubrey Gold. The name sounded expensive.

It sounded untouchable. It sounded like someone who would never again stand silently in a hallway, waiting for another person to decide whether she was safe.

Lauren believed she was preparing to become that woman. She couldn't know that reinvention would prove easier than escape. She couldn't know how many people would profit from the distance between Lauren and Aubrey, or how desperately she would later try to close it.

For now, Las Vegas remained a bright point far beyond the Alabama horizon. And in Dothan, beneath the cicadas and church bells, a young woman waited for the moment she could leave.

Dreams of Stardom

The bus station smelled of coffee, diesel, and floor cleaner. Lauren stood beneath the fluorescent lights with a bag at her feet and a ticket folded inside her purse. Around her, strangers shifted in plastic seats, half awake and guarding their luggage. An overhead speaker crackled with departure times. Somewhere beyond the glass, an engine idled in the dark.

She was eighteen years old. Behind her was Dothan, Alabama, with its church signs, peanut fields, family arguments, old judgments, and roads she could navigate without thinking.

Ahead of her was Las Vegas. Lauren had spent years imagining this moment. In those fantasies, departure felt triumphant. She would step onto the bus as one person and arrive as another. The miles between Alabama and Nevada would strip away every unwanted part of her life.

The girl who had been watched, corrected, and underestimated would disappear. Aubrey Gold would take her place.

But standing in the terminal, with departure finally close enough to touch, freedom may not have felt as clean as she had imagined. Leaving meant no grandmother waiting at home.

No familiar bedroom. No aunt in the next room.

No one nearby who knew the difference between confidence and fear when she smiled. There is a loneliness unique to getting what you thought you wanted.

Lauren picked up her bag when boarding was announced. She didn't turn back.

The decision to leave Dothan had been building for years. By the time she reached adulthood, the town no longer felt like a home she could grow within. It felt like a place she would have to escape before it decided her entire future.

Her family knew she wanted something different, but wanting something different and naming it are not the same. Lauren didn't simply want to move away.

She wanted to enter the adult film industry. That distinction changed everything.

In a conservative Southern family, such an ambition wasn't likely to be treated as an unconventional career choice. It could be experienced as rejection, shame, and betrayal all at once. Her relatives had tried to give her structure, rules, and a path toward what they understood as respectability. Lauren's plan appeared to discard all of it.

To her, the choice meant autonomy. To them, it may have looked like self-destruction.

Families often mistake control for protection when they are terrified. Young people often mistake fear for cruelty when they are desperate to leave.

Both sides can believe they are defending the same person. Once Lauren's intentions became clear, the break was severe. The exact words exchanged have been retold through memory, anger, and hurt, but the result is easier to trace.

She left. Her family withdrew.

The relationship between them fractured at the moment she needed both independence and support. This is one of the first great contradictions in Lauren's adult life. To prove she could survive on her own, she walked away from the people most likely to catch her if she fell. Her relatives may have believed that refusing support would force her to reconsider. Instead, it left her more dependent on strangers.

That dependency would become dangerous. The bus carried her west through a changing country.

The green fields and pine trees of Alabama gave way to wider roads, flatter land, and unfamiliar towns glimpsed through tinted windows. Passengers boarded and disappeared. Fast-food wrappers accumulated in seat pockets. Rest stops broke the journey into pieces measured by vending machines, cramped bathrooms, and the ache of sitting too long.

Lauren had plenty of time to think about the life she was leaving. She also had time to construct the woman she intended to become.

A stage name in the adult industry can serve several purposes. It offers privacy, branding, and distance. It allows a performer to separate the public identity being sold from the private person who must live with the consequences.

For Lauren, the name meant more. She chose Aubrey as a connection to her mother's past. Her mother had reportedly used the name during her own time working as a stripper. Taking it was both an inheritance and a revision.

Lauren could claim part of her mother's story while promising herself a different ending. Gold represented the future.

Gold was valuable. Gold drew attention.

Gold suggested that she would not remain poor, invisible, or disposable. Together, the words sounded polished and memorable.

Aubrey Gold. The name didn't carry the history of Lauren Wambles. It had never sat in a principal's office. It had never waited for an absent father or listened to relatives argue about what should be done with her. It didn't belong to Dothan.

Aubrey Gold was new. At least, that was the hope.

The closer the bus came to Nevada, the more convincing the new identity may have felt. Lauren could rehearse it silently. She could imagine introducing herself to agents, photographers, producers, and other performers.

Each repetition created distance from the girl she had been. Yet a new name can conceal history only from other people.

It can't conceal it from the person using it. Lauren carried every old wound onto the bus with her.

The abandonment. The anger. The need to be admired. The distrust of authority. The hunger for someone to confirm that she was special. All of it traveled west.

Las Vegas announces itself before a person truly enters it. The darkness of the desert gives way to an unnatural glow. Towers rise from the flat land in brilliant colors. Signs pulse above the roads. Hotels resemble palaces, cities, pyramids, castles, and fantasies borrowed from other parts of the world.

For someone arriving from Dothan, the first view must have felt impossible. Las Vegas didn't whisper about desire.

It sold desire openly. The city appeared to reject every rule Lauren had grown up beneath. Gambling, alcohol, sex, money, and spectacle weren't hidden behind closed doors. They were printed in lights several stories high.

In Las Vegas, reinvention seemed normal. That was the promise.

The reality waited several blocks beyond the Strip. Visitors see fountains, chandeliers, polished casino floors, and women walking beneath neon in glittering dresses. People who live and work in Las Vegas see another city layered behind the first one.

They see weekly motels, buses carrying casino employees home after midnight, convenience stores protected by thick glass, and apartment complexes filled with people trying to remain close enough to the fantasy to profit from it. Lauren arrived with limited money, limited experience, and no stable support system. The city didn't care how long she had dreamed of reaching it.

Rent was still due. Food still cost money.

A phone needed service. Transportation required planning.

Every day without work reduced the small distance between her and desperation. This is where the fantasy began separating from the business side of the adult industry.

From the outside, the industry appears immediate. A beautiful young woman arrives, cameras discover her, and money follows. In practice, entry depends on access.

A newcomer needs photographs, identification, health testing, contacts, transportation, and some understanding of who is legitimate. She must learn which messages are real job offers, which are unpaid "portfolio opportunities," and which are attempts to isolate her in unsafe situations.

Lauren had beauty, youth, and determination. She didn't yet have the judgment that comes from experience.

That made her attractive to more than legitimate producers. The adult industry has always contained people who offer real opportunities and others who imitate the language of opportunity. Both may call themselves agents. Both may promise exposure. Both may speak confidently about connections, rates, and future bookings.

A young newcomer often can't tell them apart. The first people who offer help can become the people with the most influence.

That influence may be protective. It may also be predatory.

Lauren entered Las Vegas at an age when legal adulthood and emotional readiness were not the same thing. The law considered her capable of signing contracts and consenting to work. The industry considered her marketable precisely because she had just crossed that legal boundary.

The difference between seventeen years and eleven months and eighteen years is enormous under the law. It is far smaller inside the mind of the person living through it.

Lauren had left home believing she was taking control. Almost immediately, she needed other people to tell her what to do next.

Where should she get photographed? Which test did she need? What rates should she accept? Who could book her? What should she bring to a shoot? Which boundaries were normal? How much questioning would make her appear difficult? Every answer carried consequences.

The first photographs attached to a new performer can shape how the industry sees her. A polished portfolio may signal professionalism. Poor images can make even a striking newcomer look unprepared.

Lauren's earliest opportunities were modest. There were no red carpets. No team waiting to transform her into a star.

There were photographers working from rented rooms, improvised studios, and private homes. Some knew how to create professional images. Others had little skill beyond convincing young women to undress for a camera.

Lauren needed material to show agents. That need weakened her ability to refuse.

This pattern appears throughout entertainment industries. A person is told she must already have experience before anyone will give her a real opportunity. To acquire that experience, she must accept the least protected work.

The first rung of the ladder is often the most dangerous. Lauren posed. The camera clicked. She learned to angle her face toward the light, arch her back, and hold expressions that suggested confidence regardless of what she felt.

This was the beginning of Aubrey Gold as a product. Lauren had always understood the power of appearance. In school, makeup and clothing had allowed her to resist the identity others assigned to her. In Las Vegas, appearance became currency.

Her body could open doors. That didn't mean she controlled what waited behind them.

She began reaching out to people in the industry and making herself available for work. The responses likely came quickly. The adult business places high value on novelty, and an attractive eighteen-year-old newcomer carries immediate commercial appeal.

Fresh face. New talent.

Barely legal. These phrases are marketing categories, but they describe a person standing at the most inexperienced point in her career.

The industry's interest can feel like validation. After years of feeling judged or ignored, Lauren suddenly encountered people telling her she had exactly what they wanted.

She was pretty enough. Young enough.

Marketable enough. The attention may have felt like proof that leaving had been the right decision.

Yet praise in a commercial setting is rarely free. When someone calls a performer beautiful, the compliment may also be a calculation. Beauty is assessed for its earning potential. Youth is treated as a temporary asset. Personality matters, but only if it can be converted into bookings and views.

Lauren wanted to be seen as exceptional. The industry saw a new commodity. Those perspectives could coexist for a time.

Her first living arrangements reflected the practical reality of arriving without resources. Young women entering entertainment often share rooms, couches, or temporary housing while waiting for work. Privacy becomes a luxury. Bags remain half packed. People come and go according to bookings, relationships, and money.

At night, Lauren may have listened to other women trade stories about shoots, agents, rates, and men they no longer trusted. The advice would have been contradictory.

Never work without being paid first. Don't upset the producers. Set firm boundaries. Be flexible or you won't get booked. Avoid drugs. Everyone parties. Save your money. You need to spend money to look successful.

For a newcomer, the industry can feel like a collection of rules that cancel one another out. Lauren had to decide whom to believe.

She had always distrusted authority, but she also craved guidance. The combination made her vulnerable to people who didn't present themselves as authority figures at all. They might act like friends, mentors, lovers, or older siblings.

Control is easier to accept when it arrives disguised as care. Not everyone she met intended to exploit her. Some people offered practical, sincere help. Experienced performers often warn newcomers about testing, unreliable producers, unsafe houses, agents who take too much money, and scenes that may exceed stated boundaries.

A makeup artist might notice fear before anyone else does. Another performer might stay close during paperwork.

A driver might refuse to leave someone at an address that felt wrong. These small acts rarely appear in documentaries about the industry, but they are part of its reality.

Lauren encountered kindness. She also encountered people who recognized exactly how alone she was.

The gap between what she imagined and what she found became apparent early. Glamour had been part of the promise.

Instead, there were forms. Freedom had been part of it too. Instead, there were instructions. Wealth had seemed close enough to touch. Instead, there were fees before the first real paycheck. Most of all, Lauren expected to control the attention of men. Instead, men often controlled access to work. Still, she pressed forward.

Returning home would have required admitting that the people who doubted her might have been right. That possibility may have felt more humiliating than any difficulty she faced in Las Vegas.

Pride can keep a person moving long after caution tells her to stop. Lauren had sacrificed too much to quit quickly.

She needed Aubrey Gold to succeed. The stage name served as more than branding; it defended her against the possibility of failure.

Lauren could be frightened. Aubrey had to be bold. Lauren could miss home. Aubrey had chosen freedom. Lauren could doubt herself. Aubrey needed to appear certain.

Performers often speak about switching into character before a shoot. The change may begin with makeup, clothing, or the use of a stage name. The public persona becomes a psychological room the performer enters.

For some, that separation is healthy. It protects privacy and helps maintain boundaries.

For others, the distance between the persona and the private self grows difficult to manage. Lauren was only beginning to discover the difference.

Her first professional experiences were unlikely to resemble the scenes she had watched as a child. Adult content is designed to look spontaneous and effortless. The set itself can be technical, repetitive, and impersonal.

Lights must be placed. Cameras must be positioned. Documents must be signed. Tests must be checked. The performer may wait for hours, then be expected to produce energy on command. Every gesture can be directed.

Every expression can be repeated. The freedom Lauren thought she had seen on screen was partly an illusion created through editing.

That realization may not have arrived all at once. Disillusionment usually comes in pieces.

A long day that paid less than expected. A boundary questioned. A ride home that cost too much. An agent who stopped answering after taking a commission.

A photograph posted without the promised credit. A man who described pressure as professionalism.

None of these events alone had to destroy the dream. Together, they began altering it.

Lauren had wanted the industry because she associated visibility with power. Now she was learning that being visible can increase vulnerability. The more people knew her face, the harder it would become to return to anonymity.

Every new scene strengthened Aubrey Gold's public identity. Every scene also narrowed Lauren Wambles' private options.

Once images are distributed online, they are difficult to contain. A performer can leave the industry, but the work may remain available indefinitely. Family members can discover it. Future employers can find it. Strangers can use it to claim intimacy with someone they have never met.

At eighteen, forever is difficult to understand. The immediate goal is rent.

The immediate reward is attention. The future remains abstract until it arrives. Lauren found moments of genuine excitement in this new life. That should not be erased.

She had left a town that made her feel trapped and reached a city she had chosen. People noticed her. She was building a name. She had crossed a boundary most people only imagined crossing.

There is power in refusing shame. There is satisfaction in earning money through a decision others said you should never make.

The adult industry didn't offer her only harm. If it had, she might have left sooner. It offered intermittent rewards powerful enough to keep her invested. A compliment from a producer.

A photograph she loved. A message from a fan. A booking that paid more than she had ever earned in one day. A night out beneath neon where she could introduce herself as Aubrey and watch people recognize the name.

Those moments made the harder parts easier to rationalize. Perhaps the next job would be better.

Perhaps the right agent would change everything. Perhaps Los Angeles would provide the opportunities Las Vegas couldn't.

Success always seemed one introduction away. This hope is common in entertainment. It survives on near misses. A performer doesn't need to be fully successful to keep going. She only needs enough evidence to believe success is close.

Lauren began to attract more attention. Her look translated well on camera. She had a youthful face, a bright smile, and the ability to appear approachable. She wasn't distant or intimidating. She carried the kind of "girl next door" image the adult market has always known how to sell.

That image contained its own irony. The girl next door was exactly what Lauren had fled. Now it formed part of her appeal.

The industry often packages rebellion in familiar forms. A performer can be presented as accessible, innocent, wild, glamorous, or dangerous depending on the audience being targeted. The person beneath the category may have little control over which version becomes most profitable.

Lauren had chosen her name. Others would help define what Aubrey Gold meant.

As bookings increased, the possibility of moving to Los Angeles became more serious. Las Vegas offered opportunity, but Southern California remained the center of traditional adult film production. More companies, agents, photographers, and performers were based there.

To advance, she would need to move again. Another city. Another reinvention. Another promise that the next place would finally match the dream. By then, leaving had become Lauren's most practiced solution. When home felt suffocating, she left Dothan.

When Las Vegas seemed limited, Los Angeles appeared to offer more. Each move provided temporary relief because distance can feel like change before a person discovers what followed her.

I think about the courage it took for an eighteen-year-old to board that bus. I also think about the danger of needing courage before acquiring judgment.

Lauren wasn't foolish for wanting a different life. She wasn't wrong to believe she deserved independence, recognition, or financial opportunity.

The tragedy lies partly in how easily those desires could be redirected by people who understood the business better than she did. What would responsible guidance have looked like at that moment?

Someone might have explained that flat-rate pay wasn't wealth. That agents required verification.

That contracts needed legal review. That images could remain public for life.

That emotional boundaries mattered as much as physical ones. That saying no to one job didn't mean losing every opportunity.

That a stage name could protect privacy but couldn't divide a person cleanly in two. Perhaps Lauren would have listened.

Perhaps she wouldn't. Young people often need to experience consequences before advice becomes real. That doesn't absolve the adults who profit from their inexperience.

By the time she prepared to leave Las Vegas for Los Angeles, Aubrey Gold was no longer merely a fantasy imagined in a Dothan bedroom. She existed.

There were photographs, bookings, industry contacts, and people who knew the name. Lauren had accomplished something significant. She had crossed the country and entered the business she had dreamed about since childhood.

But the victory was incomplete. She had escaped Alabama without escaping instability.

She had found attention without finding security. She had created a public identity without knowing whether it could protect the private person beneath it.

The lights of Las Vegas had once looked like proof that anything was possible. Soon, they began to look like another backdrop she had outgrown.

Los Angeles waited to the west, bright with new promises. Lauren packed again.

Aubrey Gold was ready for the next stage of her rise. Neither of them yet understood the price.

The Reality of the Set and the Rise of Aubrey Gold

The house looked ordinary from the street. Beige stucco. A narrow driveway. A palm tree leaning toward the roof. A dented sedan parked near the curb. Nothing about it suggested a film set.

Inside, cables crossed the floor beneath strips of black tape. A light stand blocked part of the hallway. Someone had pushed the living room furniture against the wall to make room for cameras. The air smelled of hairspray, warm electronics, and coffee that had been sitting too long.

Aubrey waited in a robe near the kitchen while a crew member adjusted the lights. She had already shown her identification.

She had already completed the paperwork. She had already compared test results with her scene partner. She had already sat for hair and makeup, changed clothes, and posed for promotional photographs. Several hours had passed.

The scene had not begun. This was the reality hidden behind the finished product.

Viewers would eventually see a polished sequence edited to appear continuous and spontaneous. They would not see the paperwork stacked on a folding table. They would not hear the director and camera operator debating angles. They would not know how long Aubrey had waited under bright lights before someone finally called her onto the set.

At twelve, she had imagined adult performers as women who controlled every room they entered. At eighteen, she was learning how often other people controlled the schedule.

"Give us ten more minutes," someone told her. Aubrey nodded and looked at her phone. Ten minutes on a film set can become forty.

The robe stayed tied around her waist. Her makeup was finished, but the day had barely started.

By the time Aubrey reached Los Angeles, she was no longer an anonymous newcomer carrying a few amateur photographs. She had begun building a recognizable name. Producers noticed her. Agents had reasons to return her calls. Her face started appearing across adult websites, promotional galleries, and scene listings.

The rise happened quickly. That speed is common in a business built around novelty. A performer can move from unknown to heavily booked in weeks if the market responds to her look. The attention creates the impression that a career is taking off before the performer has enough experience to understand where it might be going.

Aubrey had several qualities the camera rewarded. She had a youthful face, a bright smile, and an approachable quality that made her easy to market. She could appear playful without seeming distant. She had the fresh, girl-next-door image producers valued, even though she had spent years trying to escape the expectations attached to being someone's girl next door.

The contradiction was easy to miss. Lauren Wambles had left Alabama because she wanted to become unlike the girls around her.

Aubrey Gold became profitable partly because viewers could imagine she was one of them. The adult industry doesn't sell biography. It sells categories. New girl. College girl. Southern girl. Innocent girl. Wild girl.

Each label creates a fantasy while flattening the person inside it. Aubrey's life in Dothan, her family instability, her anger, her ambitions, and her fear had no value to the viewer unless they could be converted into marketing.

The camera didn't need Lauren's history. It needed Aubrey's expression.

She learned quickly. She learned where to look. She learned how to hold a pose while lighting changed. She learned how to repeat enthusiasm after the director asked for another take.

She learned to maintain the appearance of spontaneity inside a highly technical process. This is one of the least understood parts of adult production. What appears uninhibited on screen often depends on strict coordination. A legitimate set runs on identification checks, current health tests, releases, consent discussions, camera setups, and detailed instructions.

The finished scene hides the machinery. Aubrey's workday could begin early. She might receive the address the night before, along with wardrobe instructions and a call time. She would arrive carrying her own clothes, shoes, makeup, and accessories unless the company had a larger budget.

Some sets provided professional hair and makeup. Others expected performers to arrive camera-ready.

The quality of the production could be measured before the cameras rolled. A well-run set had clear paperwork, clean facilities, a professional crew, and people who respected boundaries. A questionable set might feel disorganized from the first moment, with last-minute changes and vague promises about payment.

New performers didn't always know which warning signs mattered. Even experienced performers sometimes ignored them when money was tight.

Before filming, everyone was expected to have a current industry test. During Aubrey's era, that usually meant testing every fourteen days. The panel cost approximately $155 and screened for multiple sexually transmitted infections.

The expense belonged to the performer. Testing was essential, but it was also one more cost deducted from a paycheck before the performer had paid rent, food, transportation, wardrobe, or an agent.

Miss the testing window and the performer could lose the job. Lose the job and she might not recover the testing cost.

This created a cycle outsiders rarely saw. A performer paid in advance for the ability to work, whether work arrived or not.

The test results were only part of the preparation. Each production generated documents. Identification was copied. Releases were signed. Boundaries were discussed. Performers might answer questions on camera before or after the scene to confirm age, consent, and the agreed activity.

These procedures mattered. They also revealed how different reality was from Lauren's childhood fantasy.

The adult industry she had imagined was all freedom and attention. The adult industry she entered contained administration, medical appointments, commissions, invoices, waiting, and physical labor.

The glamour existed mainly after editing. Once the paperwork was complete, the promotional photographs often came next. These still images could be used for covers, galleries, advertisements, or scene pages. A performer might spend an hour posing before the filmed work began.

She was expected to look fresh. She was expected to project energy.

She was expected to keep smiling even as the day stretched longer. The crew then reset the room.

Lights moved. Furniture shifted.

Cameras changed position. A sound issue might force another delay.

By the time the director called action, Aubrey could already be tired. The physical demands of the work were substantial, but the emotional demands were less visible. A performer had to produce convincing reactions regardless of discomfort, boredom, nervousness, or exhaustion. She had to respond to direction without allowing the direction itself to appear on screen.

That skill is work. The final edit removes the pauses, adjustments, and repetition. A viewer sees a seamless fantasy, not the performer holding a position while a camera operator searches for a better angle.

A ten-minute scene might represent hours of preparation and filming. The performer was paid once.

The company could sell the footage for years. This is where public assumptions about adult film income begin to collapse.

Mainstream audiences often imagine that performers receive royalties each time a scene is viewed or resold. In most traditional adult productions, they don't.

The performer receives a flat scene rate. When the payment clears, her financial connection to the production usually ends.

The company owns the footage. It can place the scene on a subscription site, sell it through distribution deals, repackage it in compilations, or continue monetizing it long after the performer has left the industry.

The performer receives no additional check. That fact matters because several documentaries and news reports later described Aubrey's career in ways that depended on a royalty system that didn't exist. Some claimed she had lost royalty income because of her drinking or professional problems.

The claim misunderstood the basic economics of her work. There were no ongoing royalty payments to withhold.

If Aubrey stopped booking new scenes, the money stopped. Her old work could keep earning revenue for other people.

She could still be visible everywhere and have no income arriving from any of it. Fame preserved her image while ownership kept the profits elsewhere.

The image survives. The paycheck doesn't.

Aubrey's exact rates varied by company and scene type, but the general structure of the period was consistent. A girl-girl scene might pay between $400 and $800. A boy-girl scene could bring between $600 and $1,000. More physically demanding work might pay between $1,200 and $1,400.

Those figures can sound large when separated from their context. A young woman from Alabama might hear that she could make $800 in a day and compare it to hourly wages back home. She might calculate the amount before deductions and imagine that several shoots each month would create financial independence.

The reality was less generous. An agent typically took between ten and twenty percent.

Aubrey paid for testing. She paid for transportation.

She needed clothing, shoes, cosmetics, hair products, and personal grooming. She had housing costs in expensive cities.

Some performers lived in model houses where rent was charged daily, whether they worked or not. Food still cost money.

Phones still needed service. A booking canceled at the last minute could erase an entire week's budget.

An $800 scene might become far less before Aubrey reached home. If an agent took twenty percent, $160 disappeared immediately.

Testing represented another recurring deduction. Transportation across Los Angeles could cost a significant amount, especially for performers without cars. Uber is new. For many years you had to pay a driver. Most agents had a driver on staff for the girls but they had to pay 5% of their scene fees to use him. That's another $40 gone from that $800 scene just for your ride to and from set.

The net income could fall quickly. Then there were taxes on top of all those other fees.

Adult performers were often treated as independent contractors. No employer withheld income taxes or provided health insurance, paid time off, retirement contributions, or unemployment protection.

The check looked larger because the safety net had been removed. A performer had to manage money with the discipline of a small business owner while being treated publicly as though she had simply been paid for showing up.

Many young performers entered without financial education. They didn't know how much to reserve for taxes. They didn't separate business expenses from personal spending. They didn't build emergency funds for slow periods or medical needs.

Aubrey was no exception. She was earning more money at once than she had seen in Dothan, but earning money and building stability are different skills.

The public version of Aubrey Gold required maintenance. She needed to appear successful.

That meant clothing, makeup, nights out, photographs, and a lifestyle suitable for social media. In entertainment, the appearance of momentum can create actual opportunity. Producers and agents notice who seems popular, visible, and connected.

The performer pays for that appearance. This creates a trap.

She spends money to look successful enough to attract work. She needs more work because she spent the money.

If bookings slow, the image becomes even more important and more expensive to maintain. Aubrey lived within this contradiction.

People online saw a young woman surrounded by attention. They didn't see the calculations behind the image.

She may have had hundreds or thousands of people watching her work while still worrying about rent. The myth of adult film wealth made it harder for outsiders to understand her vulnerability. A recognizable performer could be assumed to have money simply because her content was widely available.

Visibility was confused with financial security. They were not the same.

Mainstream coverage later repeated another inaccurate claim about Aubrey's career. Reporters and documentaries often said she appeared in thirty-two films, relying heavily on listings from IMDb. That figure was far below her actual output.

IMDb is not a reliable complete record of adult film work. Many adult companies never submit credits there. Independent scenes, web content, clip-store productions, and smaller companies may not appear at all.

A closer review of Aubrey's career suggests she completed approximately seventy-four scenes for established production companies and around fifty more connected to less conventional producers and so-called private collectors. Her total output was likely more than 124 scenes. Nearly four times the number repeated in many media accounts.

That difference is not minor. It changes the understanding of her career. Thirty-two credits can suggest occasional participation. More than 124 scenes across roughly two years reveal an intense schedule and a rapid accumulation of work.

Aubrey's career was brief, but it was not small. She burned through a large amount of production in a short period. The pace helps explain both her visibility and her exhaustion.

A performer can complete multiple scenes in a week, then go several weeks without a booking. The schedule is irregular, but the body remembers the work even when the bank account does not.

Aubrey's growing filmography made her look successful. Her likely total earnings tell a different story.

Using the rates common during her career, her gross income across roughly two years may have been only slightly above $50,000 before expenses. That number included all of it.

The legitimate studio scenes. The lower-tier work.

The less clearly defined private bookings. Two years of labor, exposure, physical strain, and permanent online distribution produced an income that many viewers would find unexpectedly modest.

Then the deductions began. Agent commissions. Testing. Transportation. Housing. Wardrobe. Food. Personal expenses. Taxes. Aubrey was not becoming wealthy doing porn.

She was moving money through her hands. This helps explain why performers sometimes accept work outsiders assume they could easily refuse, what some refer to as "private bookings".

The industry had more women seeking bookings than the traditional production system could employ consistently. Youth and novelty created short windows of opportunity. A performer knew another newcomer would arrive tomorrow.

Refusing a job could protect a boundary. It could also mean losing the income required to pay for the next test, the next week of housing, or the ride to another booking.

Choice still existed. But financial pressure changed its shape. This was all at a time prior to OnlyFans, where girls no longer needed to depend on studio work to survive. Back then, things were very different.

Aubrey was marketable enough to work with legitimate companies, yet legitimate studio work alone didn't always cover her expenses. The gaps between shoots mattered. The flat-rate system offered no residual income to get you through the slow periods.

Into those gaps came another category of opportunity. Private collectors.

The term could sound harmless or even flattering. A collector might describe himself as a fan seeking exclusive content for personal use. He might claim the footage would remain private. The arrangement could be presented as a custom shoot rather than an escort booking.

The distinction was sometimes real. It was also frequently manipulated.

Before direct-to-consumer platforms gave performers more control, private collectors occupied a gray area around the industry. Some created clip-store accounts or small online storefronts to make their activities appear commercial and legitimate.

A page on Clips4Sale or a similar platform could transform a private encounter into something that looked like production. The presence of a camera created distance from the reality.

A man wasn't paying for access to a performer. He was commissioning content. At least, that was how the arrangement could be described.

In practice, some of these bookings functioned as thinly disguised escort appointments. The filming might be minimal. The content might never be distributed widely (or at all). The storefront existed mainly to provide a commercial explanation for the meeting.

Agents could present these jobs as ordinary shoots. The performer needed money. The client paid more than some traditional companies. Everyone used the language most convenient to them.

This environment accounted for a substantial portion of Aubrey's output. Roughly fifty of her scenes appear connected to clip-store producers or private collector arrangements.

Not every one of those bookings was necessarily exploitative. Not every clip producer operated dishonestly. But the category created opportunities for abuse because the safeguards of a professional set could disappear. A traditional production might have a crew, documented testing procedures, a known company, and multiple witnesses.

A private booking might place a young performer alone in a hotel room or private house with a paying stranger. The money could look better because the protections had been removed.

This is another recurring pattern in labor. Risk is often disguised as higher pay.

Aubrey may have been offered $800-$1500 for an hour of work with a "collector". When rent was due, the offer could feel difficult to refuse. The collector might seem polite over messages. An agent might reassure her that the client was safe.

The performer still arrived without knowing whether the agreement would remain what she had been promised. One hour could become several. A content shoot could become an overnight expectation. A boundary could be treated as negotiable once she was already inside.

This happened to many performers during that period. The person arranging the booking might remain far away while the performer managed the consequences alone.

Aubrey's willingness to accept such work has sometimes been used as evidence of recklessness. There was recklessness in her life.

There was also economic pressure. Those realities should not be confused, but they should be considered together.

She wanted the money. She may also have felt she needed it. She'd chosen an industry that promised independence, but the payment structure kept her dependent on constant access to new work. That dependence made gatekeepers powerful.

Agents controlled introductions. Producers controlled bookings. Collectors controlled the immediate payment. Platforms controlled distribution.

Aubrey controlled less than the public image suggested. Yet she was not without power. Work still remained hers to accept or decline. Reputable companies could still become part of her professional network. Saving remained possible, at least in theory. Leaving remained possible too.

The problem was that every option carried a cost she was poorly prepared to absorb. A young performer with family support can survive a slow month.

A performer with savings can refuse a questionable booking. A performer with legal counsel can challenge a contract. A performer with reliable transportation can leave a set that feels unsafe. Aubrey had very few cushions.

Her family relationships had been damaged when she left Dothan. Her education was incomplete. Her financial habits were unstable. Her career depended on people she barely knew.

The industry didn't create every vulnerability she carried. It knew how to use them.

Aubrey's rapid rise also increased the pressure to remain relevant. The adult industry has always been driven by newness. A performer can be in high demand at the beginning of her career, then see interest fade as viewers and producers move toward someone newer.

The window can close quickly. This knowledge encourages performers to work heavily while demand remains high. Saying yes becomes a strategy.

Book as much as possible now. Earn while the attention lasts. Build the name before the market shifts.

Aubrey worked at a pace that helped establish her identity across the industry. Her fan base grew. Producers recognized her. Her scene count expanded faster than mainstream records captured.

From the outside, she was succeeding. Inside that success, exhaustion and instability grew.

A long day on set could be followed by another booking the next morning. A night out could serve as both recreation and networking. Alcohol could make social situations easier, quiet anxiety, or help separate Lauren from the work Aubrey had completed.

A substance doesn't need to begin as a crisis to become part of one. At first, drinking may have belonged to the lifestyle.

Industry parties. Clubs. Celebrations after shoots. Alcohol was available, socially accepted, and useful for numbing discomfort. The line between social drinking and dependence rarely announces itself. Friends notice missed calls.

Producers notice lateness. Makeup artists notice swollen eyes or shaking hands. The performer notices only that getting through the day feels harder without it.

Aubrey's substance issues didn't begin and end with the adult industry. Accounts from people who knew her suggest deeper problems already existed. The work gave those problems new conditions in which to grow.

She had money in bursts. She had freedom without structure. She had stress without reliable support. She had attention without intimacy. The industry didn't force her to drink. It also did little to stop her.

A production company booking a performer for one day may care primarily about whether she can complete the scene. An agent may notice a problem only when it interferes with income. Coworkers may offer concern but lack the power or knowledge to intervene.

Everyone sees a piece. No one sees the entire collapse.

During this period, Aubrey moved from Las Vegas into the larger Los Angeles market. The San Fernando Valley had long been a center of traditional adult film production. The move placed her closer to agencies, companies, and a deeper network of opportunity.

It also increased her expenses. Los Angeles offered more work but demanded more money simply to remain there.

Distances were greater. Transportation cost more.

Housing was expensive. Competition was constant.

The city was filled with people trying to become visible, each of them surrounded by others chasing the same promise. Aubrey's name helped her.

It didn't protect her. She could arrive at a set and be treated like a star for the day, then return to uncertainty when filming ended. The applause of a fan base didn't create health insurance. Recognition didn't guarantee next week's booking.

This emotional whiplash can be difficult to understand from outside the business. One day, a performer is the center of the room.

The next, no one calls. Fame becomes conditional.

Self-worth begins following the booking calendar. Aubrey had built her new identity around being wanted.

What happened when demand slowed? This question mattered more than she may have realized. The adult industry had given her what Dothan could not.

Attention. Distance.

A public identity. Money earned through her own choices.

It had also revealed that attention could be rented, distance could create isolation, and a public identity could become property owned by other people. The name Aubrey Gold appeared across more than a hundred scenes. The woman using it still lived from one payment to the next.

I have watched many performers reach this stage of a career. The early excitement remains visible, but the calculations have changed. They no longer ask only whether they can get booked.

They ask whether the booking is worth the cost. Will the agent take too much? Is the client legitimate? Will the company pay on time? How long will the day last? Can the body handle another scene? What happens if the answer is no?

For Aubrey, the answer was often to keep going. She had crossed the country to prove she could become someone else. Slowing down risked hearing Lauren's old doubts again.

She wanted success badly enough to endure the parts of the business that didn't resemble success. That determination helped her rise.

It also carried her toward people willing to exploit it. The public would later reduce her career to a few inaccurate numbers and a collection of images. Thirty-two films. A failed star. A woman supposedly deprived of royalties.

The truth was less dramatic and more revealing. Aubrey worked extensively.

She earned modestly. She paid heavily.

Her image spread farther than her income. Her career looked larger from the outside than it felt from within.

This financial and emotional imbalance didn't cause the murder that would later define her life. It didn't remove her capacity to make moral choices.

But it shaped the woman who eventually left the industry. She had entered believing performance would give her control.

She discovered a business where control was divided among contracts, agents, producers, clients, platforms, and money. The child in Dothan had watched women on a screen and seen freedom.

The young woman in Los Angeles stood beneath hot lights, waiting for someone else to call action. Her rise was real. So was the cost. And as Aubrey Gold became more visible, Lauren Wambles was growing harder to find.

Under Predatory Influence

The document looked official. A seal sat near the top. The language was dense. The formatting suggested government approval, regulation, and authority. To an eighteen-year-old performer trying to understand a complicated business, it offered exactly what it was meant to offer.

Reassurance. Aubrey held the image on her phone while someone explained that the agency was legitimate.

The paper said so. The seal said so. The person presenting it said so. What else was she supposed to believe?

New performers are often told to do their research. The advice sounds reasonable until one considers what research looks like when a young woman has no legal training, no industry mentor, limited money, and a career moving faster than her judgment can keep up.

A website can look professional. A contract can look enforceable. A certificate can look official. A predator rarely introduces himself as one. He offers opportunity. She seeks protection. In theory the relationship should work. But it doesn't always.

They speak in the language of careers, bookings, loyalty, and trust. By the time the danger becomes clear, the performer may already be financially dependent, publicly exposed, and terrified of what will happen if she tries to leave.

Aubrey's early career placed her near several people who understood that vulnerability better than she did. One of the first was Riley Reynolds.

Reynolds operated Hussie Models in Florida, presenting himself as a gateway into the adult industry for young women seeking work. His business became widely known through the Netflix documentary Hot Girls Wanted, which followed newcomers entering the industry through a Florida model house.

Hillsborough County

Riley Reynolds

Arrest Information

Full Name: Riley James Reynolds
Date: 11/19/2008   **Time:** 5.25 PM
Arresting Agency: HCSO
Arrest Location: 1402 BRANDON BL W, Hillsbourgh, FL

Personal Information

Arrest Age: 18
Current Age: 25
Gender: Male
Birthdate: 12/22/1989
Block: 800 Jerry Smith Rd
City: Dover, Florida 33527
Height: 6'01"
Weight: 175 lbs
Hair Color: BRO
Eye Color: GRN
Place of Birth: PA
Occupation: STEAK AND SHAKE PRODUCTION

Charges

#1 BURGLARY OF AN UNOCCUPIED CONVEYANCE

STATUTE: BURG0022 (3 F)

NOTES: J LOPEZ 121608

#2 GRAND THEFT THIRD DEGREE ($300   5,000)

STATUTE: THEF2001 (3 F)

NOTES: CO REL JD LOPEZ 012409

#3 CRIMINAL MISCHIEF $200 TO $1000

STATUTE: CRMS2000 (1 M)

NOTES: J LOPEZ 121608

#4 BURGLARY OF AN UNOCCUPIED STRUCTURE

STATUTE: BURG0020 (3 F)

NOTES: CO REL 01-24-09 JD LOPEZ

#5 CRIMINAL MISCHIEF $1000 OR MORE

STATUTE: CRMS3000 (3 F)

NOTES: J LOPEZ 121608

STATUTE: CRMS3000 (3 F)

NOTES: J LOPEZ 121608

The images in the documentary were not those of glamorous celebrity life. They were ordinary suburban houses. Shared bedrooms. Young women arriving with luggage and uncertain expectations. A man offering access to an industry they barely understood. The banality mattered.

Exploitation does not always occur in a dark room hidden from public view. Sometimes it operates from a ranch house on a quiet street, with paperwork on the counter and a vehicle waiting in the driveway.

Reynolds referred to young performers with language that revealed how he understood his business. He spoke of women newly old enough to perform as though they were an endlessly renewing supply.

Every day, another girl turned eighteen. The statement was practical to him.

That may be what made it so disturbing. He was not describing people reaching adulthood with individual histories, fears, and ambitions. He was describing inventory becoming legally available.

Aubrey entered the industry at precisely the age such operators valued most. Legally, she was old enough to work. Emotionally, she remained young enough to trust the wrong people.

The law draws a sharp line at eighteen. The market rushes toward the person standing just across it.

In Florida, operating a talent agency without the proper license carried serious legal consequences. Licensing rules existed to provide at least some oversight over people who recruited and placed workers.

Yet rules are only as useful as their enforcement. An agency can operate openly if no one investigates.

A contract can intimidate even when it can't survive legal scrutiny. A performer can have rights she does not know how to use.

The problem is not always the absence of law. Sometimes the law exists on paper while the person needing its protection stands alone in a motel room, unsure whom to call.

Reynolds was not hidden. His operation attracted national attention.

His methods were discussed in a documentary available to millions of viewers. Still, meaningful intervention remained limited.

What does regulation mean when the burden falls on the least powerful person to identify the violation, gather evidence, risk retaliation, and file the complaint? A young performer may be told she can report an agency. She may also be told that reporting it will end her career.

Both statements can be true. Fear of blacklisting has always been one of the industry's most effective tools of control. The adult industry is smaller than it appears from the outside. Producers, agents, performers, photographers, and directors often know one another. Reputation moves quickly.

A newcomer can believe that one powerful enemy will close every door. Even when that fear is exaggerated, it still shapes behavior.

Aubrey had already lost much of her family support when she chose the industry. She couldn't easily return home and admit the people warning her had been right. She had rent, testing fees, and daily expenses.

The people controlling access to work understood those facts. Aubrey's early exposure to questionable operators did more than create immediate risk. It taught her lessons about how power worked.

The person who broke rules might still prosper. The person harmed might be expected to remain quiet.

The contract mattered when it benefited the agent and became flexible when it inconvenienced the agent. Authority didn't always protect the vulnerable.

Sometimes authority was only a costume worn by the person exploiting them. These lessons can settle into a person without her consciously accepting them. Each compromise makes the next one easier to explain.

This is normal. Everyone does it. The industry works this way. Don't cause trouble. Take the money. Move on.

The phrase "move on" appears often around harm. It sounds like resilience. Sometimes it is merely silence with better public relations.

Aubrey continued working. One of her early scenes involved Bruno Dickems, a male performer associated with extreme content and later accused by multiple women of violent and abusive conduct.

The word "extreme" carries a dangerous ambiguity in adult production. It can refer to consensual content negotiated clearly by experienced performers.

It can also become a shield behind which coercion, pain, and boundary violations are dismissed as part of the scene. Consent to a category is not consent to everything someone chooses to do within it.

A performer can agree to rough content and still be assaulted. She can consent to one level of intensity and refuse another.

She can withdraw consent after the camera begins. These distinctions should be obvious.

On poorly controlled sets, they can be treated as inconveniences. Images circulated within the industry of a young woman with severe facial injuries after working with Bruno Dickems. Her eye was swollen. Bruising darkened the skin around it. Her lip appeared damaged.

The photographs didn't resemble stylized fantasy. They resembled evidence.

Another performer warned companies that women needed protection from men who treated abuse as entitlement. Bruno Dickems responded publicly with contempt, claiming the industry paid him to inflict that kind of harm and didn't care about the women objecting.

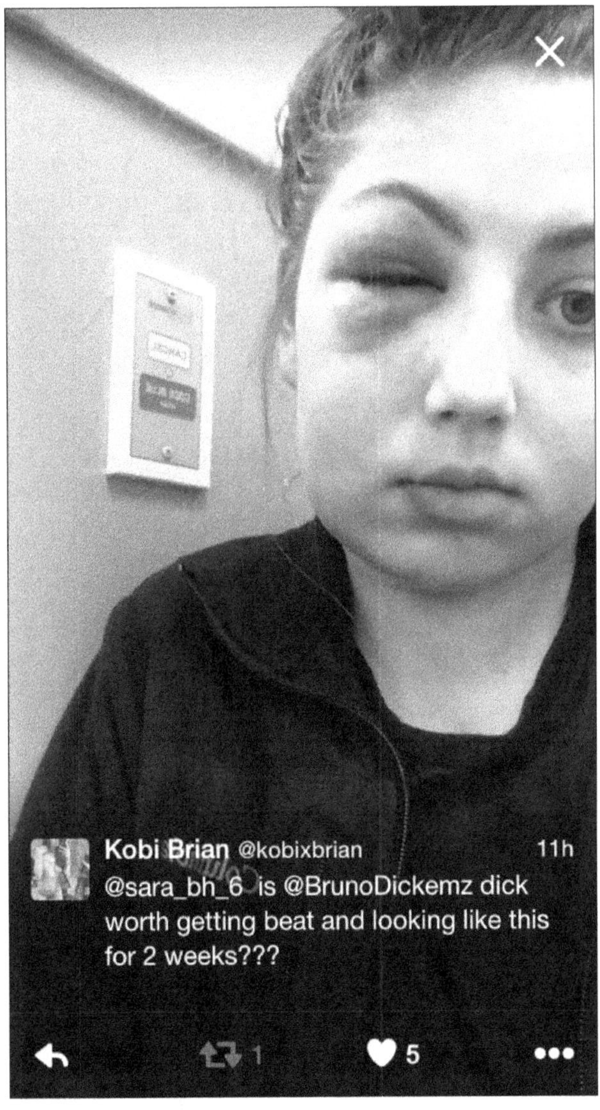
Kobi Brian @kobixbrian   11h
@sara_bh_6 is @BrunoDickemz dick
worth getting beat and looking like this
for 2 weeks???
1
5

Since were all talking about sexual assault here: when i first got into porn i lived at brunos house. One of his friends/someone i knew coerced and forced me into giving him head after i came home from dancing all night and repeatedly told him NO-

10:51 AM · Jun 3, 2020 · Twitter for iPhone

11 Retweets **99** Likes

arie $4 onlyfans @AriettaAdamsXxx · Jun 3
Replying to @AriettaAdamsXxx
Bruno barged in the door recording and i started crying and tried kicking them both while he told me if i wanted to be a pornstar this is what pornstars do! he sent the video to a group chat after that without my consent to make fun of me. fuck him and everyone who supports him

4   1   41

arie $4 onlyfans @AriettaAdamsXxx · Jun 3
I didnt realize what had happened to me was sexual assault until a year later.

11   39

The language was ugly. The attitude behind it was more important. He believed market demand excused conduct. He believed payment converted violence into professionalism. He believed the women could be ignored. The fact that someone could speak so openly suggests he didn't expect meaningful consequences. That expectation didn't arise from nowhere.

It grew from an environment in which accountability was inconsistent. One company might refuse to hire a performer accused of violating boundaries. Another might continue booking him because the content sold.

A quiet blacklist could protect some workers. It could also be applied arbitrarily, with no transparency and no reliable appeals process.

The industry had informal systems everywhere. Informal testing expectations. Informal reputation networks. Informal warnings. Informal punishments. What it often lacked was an independent structure powerful enough to act before another performer was injured.

I have spent years arguing that exploitation is not inevitable in the adult industry. The difference shaped everything that followed.

To claim abuse is simply part of the business excuses the people committing it. Many production companies operate professionally. Many directors discuss boundaries carefully. Many performers support one another and stop scenes when someone appears uncomfortable.

Ethical work exists. So does predatory work.

The danger lies in placing both beneath the same industry label and expecting a newcomer to know the difference immediately. Aubrey could arrive at one set where consent was respected and another where resistance was treated as unprofessional. The pay might be similar. The paperwork might look similar. Both companies might appear on the same industry websites.

How was she supposed to identify the threat before it revealed itself? Experience teaches recognition. Experience is often acquired through harm.

By the time Aubrey came into my orbit, she had already learned enough to know she was trapped and not enough to know how to free herself. A mutual friend contacted me about her situation with The VIP Connect.

The agency was operated by Shy Love, a former performer with a long-standing reputation inside the business. Some people viewed her as connected, aggressive, and capable of securing opportunities. Others described a pattern of control, intimidation, mismanagement, and coercion.

Aubrey wanted out. That was the simple version.

Nothing about leaving was simple. When I first spoke with her, she sounded tired before she sounded frightened. Fatigue often arrives first in situations of control. The person has repeated the story so many times, searched for so many exits, and received so many contradictory answers that fear becomes dull.

"She's not getting me work," Aubrey explained. "But she says I can't leave."

The contradiction sat at the center of the problem. An agent's purpose is to secure opportunities for the client. If the work stops, the performer's income disappears.

Yet the agency still claimed the right to control her career. The agreement reportedly bound Aubrey for years. It contained exclusivity clauses, penalties, and language designed to discourage her from seeking representation elsewhere.

Shy Love demanded a buyout. At first, the figure was around $2,500.

Later, it rose to approximately $5,000. For a performer already struggling to secure bookings, the amount was not merely inconvenient.

It was impossible. The agent was demanding money from a client whose lack of income was part of the reason she wanted to leave.

That's how a business dispute becomes a mechanism of control. Aubrey could not earn enough because the agency was not booking her.

She couldn't seek another agent because the contract claimed exclusivity. She couldn't buy her freedom because she had no money.

Each part of the arrangement strengthened the others. I asked to see the contract and whatever documentation had been used to establish the agency's legitimacy.

The papers appeared intimidating. That was part of their function.

Most young performers do not read contracts as negotiations. They read them as instructions. Dense legal wording creates the impression that every clause has been reviewed, approved, and made enforceable by someone more knowledgeable.

A signature beneath that language can feel permanent. Aubrey had signed.

That fact mattered. She was an adult.

She had a responsibility to understand what she agreed to. But a signature does not transform every contract into a valid one. Nor does it erase questions about whether the business issuing it had the legal authority to act as an agency in the relevant state.

This is where legal reality and practical reality divided. The VIP Connect was not recognized as a properly licensed California talent agency. That distinction could undermine the contract and potentially place Aubrey in a much stronger position than she realized.

In theory, she could seek relief through the California Labor Commissioner. A complaint might lead to the agreement being voided. Fees could potentially be challenged. The law offered a path.

When I explained this, Aubrey didn't look relieved. She looked afraid.

The law could tell her she was free. Shy Love could still tell producers she was unreliable, difficult, disloyal, or unstable.

In an industry where informal relationships often mattered more than written credentials, the threat felt real. "She said she'll make sure nobody books me," Aubrey told me.

I had heard variations of the same warning from many performers. I know everyone.

I'll ruin your reputation. You'll never work again.

The words are effective because they target more than employment. They target identity.

For a performer who has already sacrificed family relationships, privacy, and conventional career options, losing the industry can feel like losing the only life left available to her. Aubrey had built herself around the name Aubrey Gold. What happened if the name stopped earning money? Could Lauren return to Dothan? Would her family welcome her? Could she get an ordinary job with her porn still circulating online?

The threat of blacklisting reached far beyond the next booking. It touched every fear she had about failure.

"So there's nothing I can do?" she asked.

There was something in her posture that I have seen in other trapped performers. The shoulders move inward. The voice becomes smaller. The person who once crossed the country in defiance begins asking permission to leave a situation she never intended to remain in.

I told her there were options. I also knew options and outcomes were not the same. We could discuss filing a complaint. We could challenge the agency's licensing status. We could contact producers directly. We could document threats. But none of these steps guaranteed that retaliation would not occur. Especially since in the past Shy Love had a history of doing this to others.

This is the weakness in telling vulnerable workers simply to assert their rights. Rights require time, knowledge, emotional stamina, and often money.

A person in crisis may possess none of those. The agency relationship carried another troubling dimension. Multiple performers described The VIP Connect as more than a conventional booking agency. Some believed it facilitated escorting or private arrangements under the appearance of professional representation.

The allegation was not unique to Aubrey's experience. Women who spoke about The VIP Connect often did so anonymously. Years later, some still feared consequences. That fear is evidence of power even when it is not proof of every claim.

One performer described Shy Love's approach as a "pimp mentality." Another said the danger of a woman acting as the gatekeeper was that newcomers might assume she would protect them.

The betrayal felt different when control came from someone who understood the risks personally. Another women I spoke with, worked as a performer knew how vulnerable a newcomer could be.

She knew how reputation functioned. She knew how financial desperation narrowed choices. She knew what threats would be most effective. That knowledge could be used to protect. It could also be weaponized. Women do not become safe merely because they are women.

Shared gender does not guarantee solidarity. Sometimes it creates trust that a predator can exploit more efficiently.

Aubrey's position worsened as bookings slowed. She took part-time work assisting an older, wealthy man, an attempt to create income outside the scenes she was no longer getting consistently.

The job didn't solve the larger problem. Her expenses remained high.

The public image of Aubrey Gold required money. Rent, clothing, beauty maintenance, nightlife, and transportation continued even as earnings became irregular.

She was caught in the familiar entertainment trap of appearing successful while becoming increasingly unstable. As her security weakened, the image mattered more.

Every dollar spent maintaining it weakened that security further. Alcohol moved deeper into that cycle.

At first, drinking can make the room easier. It loosens conversation.

It softens fear. It allows someone to enter a party alone and behave as though she belongs there.

For Aubrey, alcohol increasingly served more than a social purpose. It offered a way to endure.

Industry events required performance even when no cameras were present. A performer was expected to be charming, visible, and available for conversation. Producers watched. Agents watched. Other performers watched.

A bad night could become a story. A good night could become a booking.

Aubrey began arriving already intoxicated. Her laughter grew louder.

Her frustration spilled into public view. The control she had struggled to maintain slipped in front of the people deciding whether she would work again.

I remember one event where her makeup was smudged and her dress looked as though she had slept in it or pulled it from the floor. She spoke openly about her problems with Shy Love, saying more than was safe in a room built on gossip.

People noticed. Concern and judgment can look similar from across a crowded room. Some friends tried to help her. Others kept their distance. Industry professionals made quiet calculations about reliability. Could she arrive on time? Could she complete a scene? Would she create problems on set?

Each question affected future income. The drinking that helped Aubrey numb the fear of losing work made her more likely to lose work.

This is how spirals tighten. The behavior created by panic produces the outcome the person fears.

Then the outcome appears to justify more drinking. A missed shoot carries a direct cost for a production company. Locations, crew, equipment, and scene partners have already been scheduled. Producers remember performers who fail to arrive.

The industry can be compassionate in private and unforgiving in practice. A friend may understand addiction.

A company still has to finish the scene. Aubrey's name began carrying two reputations.

To fans, she remained young, beautiful, and desirable. To some people behind the scenes, she was becoming risky.

The split between public image and private deterioration widened. This is one reason fame can conceal crisis so effectively. The old scenes remain online. Promotional photographs continue circulating. Fans keep sending praise.

The person can appear frozen at her most polished even as her real life falls apart. Aubrey's image was still working.

Aubrey was working less. Lauren was drinking more.

I've often wondered whether I could have done more during that period. It's easy to look backward and identify the moment when concern should have become intervention. In real time, the boundaries are less clear.

Aubrey was an adult. She made decisions. She could accept or refuse help.

Advocates are not family members, therapists, police officers, or judges. We can explain rights, make calls, share resources, and stand beside someone.

We can't force her to choose safety. Nor should we pretend that forcing a vulnerable person is always protection. Many performers have already experienced too many people making decisions on their behalf.

The line between intervention and control can be painfully thin. Still, the questions remain.

Should someone have insisted she enter treatment? Should a producer have stopped booking her sooner? Should friends have contacted her family?

Would her family have helped, or would the shame surrounding her career have made everything worse? What does help look like when the person needing it distrusts nearly every form of authority?

I don't know. I know only that we recognized pieces of the danger without seeing where they would eventually lead.

Aubrey's contract dispute didn't cause the murder of Raul Guillen. Shy Love didn't determine Aubrey's future. Riley Reynolds and Bruno Dickems didn't create every wound she carried.

Causation is not that simple. But these encounters formed part of the environment through which she learned to move. They taught her that official-looking systems could be fraudulent.

They taught her that people in authority might exploit rather than protect. They taught her that fear could be used as a business tool.

They taught her that pain might be dismissed if money was involved. They taught her to survive the immediate situation and postpone the emotional cost.

Those lessons followed her after the cameras stopped. A vulnerable person exposed repeatedly to control may become more skilled at recognizing it.

She may also become more likely to accept it as normal. Aubrey had spent years chasing autonomy and repeatedly entered relationships that reduced it.

An agent promised opportunity and created dependence. A contract promised representation and became confinement.

Alcohol promised relief and became another form of control. The pattern would repeat later with a man who promised protection.

By then, the stakes would be much higher. Toward the end of one of our conversations, Aubrey asked me a question that sounded practical but carried more weight than she may have realized.

"What do I do now?" She was asking about an agent. She was also asking about money, identity, and the future she had built around a career slipping away from her.

I gave her the best answers I had. Document everything.

Understand the licensing issue. Do not let threats become facts without challenging them.

Protect your reputation where possible. Find income that does not depend on the people controlling you.

The advice was sound. It was not enough.

Advice can't replace stability. Knowledge can't erase addiction.

A legal remedy can't heal the fear that made the threat effective. Aubrey left the conversation with options.

She didn't leave with a new life. Soon, her career would begin closing around her. Friends would remember both her warmth and her chaos. Private bookings would expose her to more dangerous situations. Drinking and drugs would become harder to separate from daily survival.

The young woman who had once boarded a bus believing no one would control her again was now asking strangers how to escape another person's authority. The answer remained possible. The exit remained open.

But Aubrey was already exhausted, frightened, and running out of money. And sometimes an open door is useless when the person trapped behind it no longer believes she can reach it.

Complex Perspectives and the Transition Out

The birthday set didn't look like the beginning of a tragedy. There was laughter between takes, music playing somewhere beyond the lights, and the loose energy that settles over a production when everyone knows the day is supposed to feel celebratory.

Aubrey had turned nineteen. For one scene, she was allowed to choose her co-star. She chose Kendra Cole.

Years later, when Kendra remembered that day, she didn't describe a cold or calculating young woman. She remembered warmth. She remembered an easy sense of fun. She remembered Aubrey telling stories between setups and moving through the room with a brightness that made other people want to be near her.

"She was like a bright ray of sunshine," Kendra told me. "A ball of fantastic energy and warmth. You couldn't help but love her."

That memory matters. It does not absolve Aubrey of anything that came later. It does not erase the drinking, the drugs, the manipulation, the crime, or the choices that placed Raul Guillen in danger.

It matters because human beings are more than the worst thing they eventually do. The young woman laughing on her nineteenth birthday and the woman later sentenced to prison were the same person.

That's difficult for people to hold. True crime prefers cleaner lines.

A villain should have always been cruel. A victim should have always been innocent.

A person headed toward disaster should show signs that become obvious in retrospect. But the people who knew Aubrey didn't remember one consistent version of her.

They remembered several. Kendra remembered the sunshine.

Others remembered chaos. Both were telling the truth.

Aubrey could be affectionate, funny, and generous with her attention. She could also be volatile, intoxicated, destructive, and impossible to reach.

The contradiction unsettled those around her because they could see the person worth protecting and the person creating danger at the same time. One industry acquaintance, whom I will identify only as SS, entered the business around the same period as Aubrey. Her memories were less gentle.

"She drank too much," SS told me. "A lot. Sometimes hotel rooms ended up destroyed. She was sweet, but she was a mess."

The phrase carried affection and exhaustion in equal measure. A mess.

It is a common description for someone whose pain has become inconvenient to everyone nearby. The words can sound dismissive, but they often come from people who have already tried to help. They have cleaned up the room, found the missing phone, called the driver, calmed the argument, and stayed awake to make sure the person kept breathing.

Then it happens again. Compassion wears down into fatigue.

Fatigue creates distance. Aubrey's drinking was not an invisible private habit. It left evidence.

Empty bottles. Missed commitments.

Damaged rooms. Conversations forgotten by morning.

Friends learning to read her condition before deciding whether they could leave her alone. A hotel room after one of her episodes may have looked like the physical version of an internal collapse. Clothing scattered across the floor.

Makeup broken against a bathroom counter. A lamp tilted. A door damaged. The air stale with alcohol and anger.

Temporary rooms can become dangerous places for people without stable homes. They belong to no one.

They carry no family history. Inside a temporary room, consequences can feel as disposable as the key card. They are not.

The charges do not disappear. Neither do the memories.

SS believed that the money Aubrey earned made some of her problems worse. The income was not substantial enough to create long-term stability, but it arrived in bursts large enough to fund impulsive decisions.

A few hundred dollars could pay for substances before it paid for savings. A larger booking could become a night out.

Money that should have purchased distance from danger sometimes bought a faster return to it. Financial independence does not automatically produce safety. Money often amplifies the habits and circumstances already surrounding its recipient.

For someone with support, planning, and stable routines, income can create freedom. For someone struggling with addiction and emotional instability, it can make self-destruction easier to finance.

That does not mean Aubrey should have been denied control over her earnings. It means control without preparation can become another test a vulnerable person is expected to pass alone.

I have watched young performers receive more money in one day than they had previously earned in a week. They celebrate, buy clothes, cover friends' expenses, and assume another booking will arrive before the money runs out.

Sometimes it does. Sometimes the phone remains silent.

The adult industry does not provide a predictable paycheck. There is no guarantee of hours next week. No unemployment claim when a producer stops calling. No paid leave when the body or mind needs rest.

The performer may be earning while also falling. From the outside, the money hides the fall.

Another acquaintance, whom I will call B, described a night in 2016 at a party hosted by the music duo Rae Sremmurd. The setting should have represented everything Lauren once imagined success would look like.

Music. Celebrity.

A crowded house. The feeling of being close to people the wider world recognized.

Instead, Aubrey ended up hiding inside a closet. She had taken drugs.

She was crying and screaming. Friends tried to coax her out, but she would not come.

The party around her stalled as the situation grew more disruptive. Eventually, the hosts wanted everyone associated with her removed from the house.

The image stays with me. Aubrey had entered the adult industry because she wanted to be seen.

At a celebrity party, surrounded by noise and attention, she retreated into darkness and could not be reached. The closet became a refuge from the very world she had chased.

What happened inside her mind in that moment? Was she frightened by something real? Was she hallucinating? Had old memories surfaced? Was she simply overwhelmed by a mixture of substances, exhaustion, and panic?

We can't know. What we do know is that people around her saw a crisis and lacked the tools to resolve it.

They were friends, acquaintances, performers, and party guests. They were not addiction specialists.

They could ask her to come out. They could sit near the door.

They could try to keep the situation from becoming worse. Then the night ended, and everyone returned to their own lives.

Crisis intervention is not treatment. The distinction matters.

A person may be rescued from a closet and remain trapped in the larger pattern that put her there. Aubrey's substance use is often presented as a consequence of her work in the adult industry. The timeline is more complicated. People who knew her described problems that were already present and then intensified as her career progressed.

The industry didn't place every wound inside her. It gave the wounds new places to open.

It brought irregular income, constant judgment, physical labor, late nights, and social environments where alcohol and drugs were readily available. It also provided friendship, pride, work, and moments of genuine enjoyment.

Reducing the business to either salvation or destruction misses the point. For Aubrey, it was an environment.

What she carried into that environment shaped what it became. As her substance use worsened, the gap between the two Aubreys widened.

On a good set, she could still be charming. She could laugh, perform, and make coworkers feel close to her.

On another night, she could become frightened, destructive, or detached. People who met only one version sometimes doubted the stories told by those who had seen the other.

This happens often around addiction. The person can appear functional enough to discredit the severity of the problem.

She arrives on time once. She looks beautiful.

She completes the work. She answers messages politely.

Then someone else encounters her two days later and finds her incoherent. Both experiences are real.

Addiction does not erase personality all at once. It interrupts it.

The person everyone loves continues appearing often enough to make change seem possible. That hope keeps friends involved longer than they might otherwise remain.

It can also delay the moment when everyone recognizes how serious the problem has become. Aubrey's growing instability affected her professional choices.

Traditional scene work had never produced the wealth outsiders imagined. As bookings became less consistent, she needed additional income.

Some performers solved that problem through feature dancing, live appearances, cam work, or content sales. Others accepted private bookings.

For Aubrey, those private arrangements increasingly blurred the boundary between filming and escorting. Escorting has existed alongside the adult film industry for decades, though the two are not interchangeable. Most adult performers do not automatically escort, and performing in films should not be treated as evidence that someone does.

Yet some performers supplement their income through private companionship or sexual services. During Aubrey's career, agents sometimes arranged those bookings.

The arrangement could be described using softer language. A private.

A party. A collector shoot.

A dinner date. A custom session.

The words changed depending on who was speaking and how much legal distance they wanted from the transaction. What mattered was what happened once the performer arrived.

One woman I will identify as RL worked a private booking with Aubrey. The agreement was supposed to be simple.

Two performers. One client. Approximately one hour. A payment of $1,800.

When they arrived, the terms changed. The client expected an overnight session. He wanted them to remain and party for hours. The one-hour booking had become something else after they were already present.

This tactic is common in exploitative arrangements. The client presents one set of expectations during negotiation, then expands them once the performer has traveled, entered the location, and committed psychologically to receiving the payment.

Leaving is still possible. It is not always easy. The performer may fear losing the money. She may be far from home. The agent may pressure her to stay. The client may become angry.

A colleague's willingness to remain can become the only immediate protection available. RL remembered Aubrey's reaction as strangely indifferent.

Aubrey didn't seem outraged by the change. She seemed resigned.

She was there for the payment, whether the appointment lasted one hour or all night. That resignation frightened RL more than anger might have.

Anger suggests the person recognizes a boundary has been violated. Resignation can suggest she has stopped expecting boundaries to matter.

RL stayed because she didn't feel comfortable leaving Aubrey alone. "There was an innocence to her," she told me. "You wanted to protect her."

The comment echoed what I heard repeatedly from people who knew Aubrey. She made people want to protect her.

This was not because she always behaved helplessly. In some circumstances, she could be bold, confrontational, and demanding.

Yet beneath that surface, others sensed that she didn't fully understand the danger around her. Or perhaps she understood it and no longer believed she could avoid it.

Those are different conditions. They can look the same from across a room.

RL's memory raises difficult questions about consent under changing economic pressure. Aubrey had agreed to attend the booking.

She had agreed to receive the payment. When the client expanded the expectations, she may have decided the money was worth staying.

That decision was still hers. But how free is a decision made after the terms have shifted, the performer has arrived, and financial need is pressing?

Consent can exist inside pressure. That does not make the pressure irrelevant.

Too often, public discussions force a false choice. Either the performer agreed and therefore no exploitation occurred, or she was exploited and therefore had no agency.

Reality is more complicated. Someone may knowingly accept an arrangement that still takes advantage of her.

She can accept unfair terms because her alternatives are worse. She can participate willingly while still being manipulated.

Recognizing exploitation does not require pretending she made no choices. Recognizing choice does not require pretending the surrounding conditions were fair.

Aubrey's private bookings helped maintain the appearance that her career was financially successful. They also placed her in spaces with fewer protections.

A studio set usually included other performers and crew members. A private session might involve only the client, the performer, and whoever came with her.

There was no production manager watching the clock. No formal process for stopping.

No established company reputation to protect. If the agreement changed, enforcement depended largely on the performer's ability to leave.

For a young woman struggling with substances, money, and boundaries, that was a dangerous position. Aubrey's agent reportedly arranged some of these meetings. That detail complicates the idea of professional representation.

An agent should negotiate opportunities and protect the client's interests. When the opportunity itself creates risk, the agent's financial incentive may conflict with the performer's safety.

The agent receives a percentage. The performer enters the room.

That physical difference matters. The person arranging a private booking can remain on the phone, promising everything is legitimate.

The performer absorbs the consequences if it is not. By this point, Aubrey's career was becoming unsustainable from several directions at once.

Her body was tired. Her finances were unstable. Her drinking damaged reliability. Her drug use intensified emotional volatility.

Her relationship with representation left her feeling trapped. Private work exposed her to situations where the agreed boundaries could change without warning.

The public still saw Aubrey Gold. The people around her increasingly saw Lauren struggling to hold the persona together.

She had built Aubrey as a path toward control. Now the name had become another obligation.

Fans expected availability. Producers expected reliability. Agents expected commission. Clients expected access.

The person beneath those expectations had fewer places to retreat. Leaving the industry didn't happen through one clear decision.

There was no final set where Aubrey removed her makeup, looked into the mirror, and calmly decided she was finished. Careers often end more quietly.

The bookings slow. Calls go unanswered. One absence becomes several. Reputation changes. The performer accepts less desirable work, then begins avoiding work altogether. At some point, the career exists more in archived scenes than in the person's daily life.

Aubrey's departure developed through exhaustion and diminishing options. She had entered the business quickly and worked extensively. More than 120 scenes across roughly two years represented a compressed amount of exposure and labor.

The pace was difficult to sustain even for someone with stable mental health and strong financial discipline. Aubrey had neither.

She had come to the industry seeking attention, autonomy, and escape. Attention became pressure.

Autonomy became dependence on gatekeepers. Escape became another unstable life she didn't know how to leave.

The physical fatigue was only part of it. Adult performance requires a person to be present inside the body while also treating the body as a work instrument. Boundaries must be monitored. Expressions must be produced. Discomfort must be evaluated against the need to finish the scene.

For someone using substances, that relationship with the body can become more fragmented. Alcohol and drugs may dull pain, reduce anxiety, or make difficult work feel manageable.

They also weaken judgment. A performer may accept a booking she would otherwise refuse.

She may overlook a warning sign. She may wake the next day with incomplete memories of what happened.

The substances that help her get through the work can make future work more dangerous. This does not mean every performer uses drugs or needs them to perform. Most do not. Many are disciplined professionals who protect their health carefully.

Aubrey's problems were her own. The industry's failure was not that it created them.

The failure was that so many people could see pieces of the crisis without a dependable system for responding. A producer might stop booking her.

An agent might threaten her. A friend might stay through the night. A coworker might drive her home. None of those responses addressed the addiction itself. There was no department requiring an assessment. No paid leave. No employer-sponsored rehabilitation program. No stable human resources structure.

The adult industry often classifies performers as independent contractors, which means the person can be surrounded by businesses while remaining institutionally alone. Independence sounds empowering until the person needs help. Then it can mean everyone denies responsibility.

I have asked myself where intervention should have occurred. When she destroyed a hotel room?

When she missed a shoot? When she hid in the closet? When a colleague refused to leave her with a client? How many visible emergencies must happen before concern becomes action?

The answer seems obvious in retrospect. In the moment, each incident can be treated as separate. A bad night. A difficult booking. Too much alcohol. An unfortunate reaction. A performer acting unprofessionally. Only later do the events form a line. That line now appears to point directly toward catastrophe. At the time, it did not.

Many people struggle, leave the industry, get sober, and rebuild their lives. Aubrey still had other futures available.

She could have entered treatment. She could have found different work. She could have returned home and repaired family relationships. She could have connected with people willing to help her transition.

The existence of those possibilities makes what happened later more painful, not less. A tragic outcome can make every previous warning feel like destiny.

It wasn't destiny. It was risk accumulating.

The decision to leave the adult industry may have brought Aubrey temporary relief. She no longer had to maintain the production schedule or face the constant evaluation of her body and marketability.

But leaving removed one of the few structures still organizing her life. Even an unstable career provides call times, payments, obligations, and an identity.

Without it, she had to answer questions she had spent years avoiding. Who was Lauren Wambles without Aubrey Gold? Where could she work? How could she explain the gap in her education and resume? Could she live in Los Angeles without bookings? Could she return to Dothan after leaving so defiantly? Would her family see her return as a request for help or proof of failure?

Performers leaving the industry often discover that the stigma remains after the income ends. The scenes stay online. The name remains searchable. Strangers continue consuming an identity the performer no longer inhabits.

She may apply for conventional work knowing an employer could discover everything with a few keystrokes. She's expected to transition quietly into a society that has documented the part of her life it is least willing to forgive.

Aubrey had no clear bridge between the two worlds. The industry didn't offer an exit plan.

Dothan didn't offer anonymity. Her family support remained uncertain.

Her grandmother, the person who had once provided the most stable home, was no longer a permanent safety net. The road back to Alabama began to look less like a choice than an admission that every other option had failed.

I think of Kendra's memory often. Aubrey on her nineteenth birthday.

Laughing. Choosing a coworker she liked.

Moving through the day with warmth. That version of her was real.

So was the young woman screaming inside a closet. So was the performer who stayed at a private booking after the terms changed.

So was the friend people wanted to protect. So was the adult who repeatedly made decisions that placed herself and others in danger.

There is no single image that explains her. Perhaps that's why the media preferred the mugshot.

A mugshot simplifies. It removes movement, laughter, contradiction, and context. It gives the viewer one face and one implied conclusion. Guilty. Dangerous. Fallen.

The memories of her coworkers offer no such certainty. They leave us with a woman who could inspire love and alarm in the same person.

A woman who appeared worldly but remained naive. A woman who wanted independence and repeatedly entered situations where other people controlled the terms.

A woman who earned attention but could not convert it into safety. By the time she stepped away from the adult industry, Aubrey had little money to show for the work, a damaged reputation, worsening substance use, and no clear future.

The career had not made her wealthy. It had not made her secure.

It had not transformed Lauren into someone untouched by her past. The stage name remained online, bright and permanent.

The woman behind it was preparing to return to Alabama. She had once boarded a bus believing Dothan was the life she needed to escape.

Now it was one of the last places left to go. The return would not restore the girl she had been. Her grandmother's home would no longer offer the same refuge. The town would remember her departure.

Lauren would return carrying the public history of Aubrey Gold, the private weight of addiction, and the knowledge that the future she had risked everything to build was already collapsing behind her. The cameras had stopped. The consequences had not.

Return to Dothan and the Downward Spiral

The Alabama heat met her before the terminal doors closed behind her. It pressed against her skin with the thick familiarity of childhood, heavy with humidity, asphalt, and distant rain. Somewhere beyond the airport, pine trees lined the roads toward Dothan. Gas stations, church signs, low shopping plazas, and fields waited in the same places they had occupied before she left.

Lauren stood with her luggage beside her. Aubrey Gold had returned home.

There was no crowd waiting. No celebration.

No proof that the years away had produced the life she once promised herself. The woman who came back carried more than clothes. She brought the searchable history of her career, debts she couldn't easily pay, a worsening dependence on drugs and alcohol, and the humiliation of returning to the place she had been determined to escape.

She had left Dothan believing departure would divide her life into before and after. The before belonged to Lauren Wambles.

The after would belong to Aubrey Gold. Now the two identities arrived at the same terminal with nowhere left to separate them.

Returning home can be harder than leaving. The streets are familiar, but the person moving through them is not. Every building contains an earlier version of the self. A convenience store is not just a place to buy cigarettes. It's where an old classmate works. A grocery aisle becomes a reunion. A traffic light holds the memory of riding in someone else's car before the future had narrowed.

In Los Angeles, Aubrey had been one performer among many. In Dothan, Lauren was the local girl who had gone away to make porn. Small towns preserve stories. They do not always preserve mercy.

People may not have said anything directly when they recognized her. They didn't need to. A glance held too long could say enough. A lowered voice after she passed could reopen every wound she had tried to bury beneath the stage name.

Some people may have looked at her with pity. Others with curiosity. A few with satisfaction.

She had left believing she was better than the life Dothan offered. Now she had returned without the wealth, fame, or stability that might have silenced those who doubted her.

Failure becomes more painful when witnesses are waiting. Lauren needed a place to land. For much of her childhood, that place had been her grandmother's home.

Shirley Wambles had given her structure when her parents could not. The house had contained rules Lauren resented, but it also contained meals, clean clothes, routine, and the knowledge that someone would still be there when morning came.

By the time Lauren returned, that safety was gone. Her grandmother had died.

The loss was larger than the death of one relative. It removed the person and place most closely associated with stability in Lauren's life. The home she once experienced as controlling could no longer receive her.

Grief often changes the meaning of memory. The rules that once felt restrictive can begin to look like care.

The bedroom that seemed too small can become the room a person would give anything to enter again. Lauren had spent years trying to escape her grandmother's control.

Now she returned to a world without it. She moved in with her aunt. The arrangement gave her shelter, but shelter and stability are not the same.

She was no longer a child whose relatives could organize her days. She was an adult carrying addiction, shame, and a public identity that followed her into every room. Her aunt could offer a place to sleep. She couldn't restore the years before Las Vegas or erase what had happened in Los Angeles.

Living with family may also have intensified Lauren's sense of regression. She had once lived independently in cities built around reinvention. She had earned money through work most people in Dothan could barely discuss without judgment. She had been recognized by strangers, photographed, booked, and desired.

Now she depended on relatives again. The contrast must have been unbearable.

When pride is the last possession left, even help can feel humiliating. Lauren had few conventional employment options.

Her education had ended before graduation. Her work history could not be placed easily on an ordinary application. Even if she omitted it, the name Aubrey Gold remained one search away.

Former performers often discover that leaving the industry does not end the stigma attached to it. The scenes remain online after the income stops. Employers can reject them quietly. Landlords can treat them differently. Banks, payment companies, and service providers may close accounts or deny access.

The public continues consuming the work while condemning the person who made it. Lauren returned to a region with limited opportunity even for people who didn't carry her history.

She had no degree. No savings. No stable career. No clear plan. The structure of work had disappeared, and nothing replaced it.

Without call times, travel schedules, tests, and bookings, her days loosened. Time became harder to measure. The routines that had once forced her to show up, even imperfectly, were gone.

Addiction thrives in unstructured hours. The drinking and drug use that had disrupted her career followed her home. Returning to Alabama didn't remove the pain she had tried to numb in California. It placed her back among the memories that helped create it.

The substances offered temporary distance. They also brought her closer to people living outside ordinary systems of work and accountability.

As Lauren's dependency worsened, legal trouble followed. Court records show a rapid series of arrests. Drug possession. Receiving stolen property. Other offenses tied to a life becoming increasingly unstable. Six arrests accumulated in a relatively short period.

Each arrest reduced her options further. A criminal charge creates consequences before any prison sentence begins. Court dates interrupt work. Fees accumulate. Probation rules create new opportunities for violation. Employers grow more reluctant. Housing becomes harder to secure.

The person turns toward the people who will still accept her. Those people may be struggling inside the same world.

The mugshots from this period tell a story that numbers can't. In one image, traces of the young performer remain.

In another, exhaustion settles deeper into her face. The eyes lose focus.

The expression hardens or empties. A mugshot records only a fraction of a second, but a sequence of them can reveal deterioration no single photograph contains.

The camera that once sold Aubrey's youth now documented Lauren's collapse. There were no stylists.

No flattering light. No one directing her to lift her chin.

Only a wall, a booking number, and the state's record of another arrest. It is tempting to view those photographs as proof that her criminal path had become inevitable.

It had not. Many people are arrested during periods of addiction and later recover.

Many return home after failed careers and rebuild. Many lose family members without entering violent criminal circles.

Lauren's circumstances increased her vulnerability. Her decisions still mattered.

At each stage, another path remained possible. Treatment. Work. Distance from the people supplying her drugs. Repairing family relationships. A move to another city. None would have been easy. Difficulty is not the same as impossibility.

But addiction changes how possibilities appear. Immediate relief becomes more important than distant stability.

The next hour matters more than next year. The person begins organizing life around avoiding withdrawal, finding money, locating substances, and maintaining relationships with whoever can provide them.

Moral boundaries do not always collapse dramatically. They erode through repetition. A stolen item becomes money. A dishonest explanation becomes necessary. A dangerous person becomes useful. The unacceptable becomes familiar. A producer once described Aubrey to me in words I have never forgotten.

"A predator's dream." The phrase was cruel in its precision.

She was attractive, emotionally vulnerable, financially unstable, hungry for protection, and accustomed to confusing attention with care. She could appear experienced while remaining easy to manipulate.

Predators do not always seek helpless people. They often seek people who believe they are too experienced to be fooled.

Lauren had spent years around agents, producers, clients, and men who tested boundaries. She may have believed she understood dangerous personalities.

Familiarity can create false confidence. It can also normalize behavior that should trigger fear.

By the time William Shane Parker entered her life, Lauren was no longer the eighteen-year-old newcomer stepping off a bus in Las Vegas. She had been through contracts, private bookings, addiction, public exposure, financial collapse, and arrest.

She knew the world could be cruel. That didn't mean she knew how to protect herself from cruelty offered as love.

Shane was older than Lauren by more than a decade. He carried the physical presence and local reputation of someone accustomed to intimidation. People around him understood that violence was not merely something he talked about.

It was part of how he moved through the world. To an emotionally stable person, these qualities might have appeared as warnings.

To Lauren, they may have looked like protection. She had spent much of her life seeking someone stronger than the chaos around her.

Her father had not provided that security. Agents had promised to guide her and instead created dependence.

Friends could protect her for one night but not rebuild her life. Shane offered something more immediate.

He could make other people afraid. For a woman who had spent years feeling exposed, another person's capacity for violence could be mistaken for safety.

The relationship began while both were incarcerated on unrelated charges. Their connection developed through letters.

There is an intimacy peculiar to correspondence from jail. The writer has time. The page becomes a place to confess, exaggerate, promise, and imagine a future untouched by the circumstances surrounding the present.

Lauren wrote to Shane. He wrote back.

Words passed between two confined people who may have felt that no one else understood them. The relationship formed before they had to navigate ordinary life together.

There were no shared bills. No public arguments.

No days spent discovering each other's habits outside controlled visiting schedules and written pages. Each could present a carefully shaped self.

Shane could become the protector. Lauren could become the woman worth protecting.

Both roles carried emotional rewards. For Lauren, the letters may have felt safer than the relationships she had known. A man behind bars could not disappear for the night, arrive unexpectedly, or physically control the room.

Distance created the illusion of emotional honesty. It also left space for fantasy.

Letters can invite disclosures that ordinary conversation does not, but disclosure is not the same as truth. Shane could sincerely describe the man he wanted to be while remaining dangerous in practice.

When Lauren and Shane were released, the imagined relationship entered the physical world. They became inseparable.

That intensity may have felt romantic. It was also isolating.

Witnesses later described Shane as controlling and rarely apart from Lauren. Constant presence can be presented as devotion.

We do everything together. I can't stand being away from you.

I only trust you. The language sounds intimate.

It can also eliminate the space necessary for independent judgment. Control does not always begin with threats.

It begins with attention. The person calls constantly because she matters.

He wants to know where she is because he worries. He dislikes certain friends because they do not respect the relationship.

He handles problems because she has already suffered enough. Each step can feel like care until the person realizes she's asking permission to move.

Lauren may have welcomed Shane's possessiveness. Being claimed can feel like being valued to someone who has spent years being treated as temporary.

The adult industry had taught her that attention was conditional. Fans wanted the image. Producers wanted the scene. Clients wanted access. Their interest ended when the transaction did.

Shane's interest appeared personal. He wanted Lauren, not just Aubrey.

Or perhaps he wanted the status of possessing Aubrey Gold while controlling Lauren Wambles. Both may have been true.

To Shane, her past could have increased her value and intensified his jealousy. She had been desired by thousands of strangers. Being the man who now controlled her could feed both pride and insecurity.

Possession is not love. It can resemble love closely enough to trap someone desperate for it.

Lauren's relationship with Shane deepened within a world shaped by methamphetamine. The drug changes sleep, appetite, perception, and judgment. Extended use can produce paranoia, agitation, delusions, impulsivity, and emotional extremes.

Relationships formed around methamphetamine often develop an artificial intensity. Hours pass without sleep.

Conversations feel profound. Suspicion becomes certainty.

Jealousy becomes evidence. Shared use creates a closed world in which the people inside reinforce one another's distorted thinking.

Lauren and Shane didn't simply use drugs near each other. Their life began organizing itself around them.

The relationship and the addiction strengthened one another. Shane's violent reputation provided access and protection within criminal circles.

Lauren's attachment made it harder for her to question him. Together they entered the orbit of Jeremie Odell Peters.

He was known as JP. JP presented himself through the appearance of legitimate work. He operated a construction business, but court records and witness accounts linked him to drug dealing.

The construction company offered a useful front. Vehicles moved.

Workers came and went. Cash could be explained.

People with unstable histories could be employed without many questions. Behind that surface, JP allegedly supplied drugs and maintained control through debt, intimidation, and people willing to enforce his demands.

Shane became one of those people. He served as muscle.

The role suited him. Violence gave him status.

JP needed someone who could frighten people. Shane needed someone whose operation gave that aggression purpose.

Each benefited from the other. Lauren entered the arrangement through Shane.

By then, her social world had narrowed sharply. She was no longer surrounded by performers, makeup artists, producers, and industry parties. The people around her were increasingly connected through drugs, arrests, debts, and informal criminal relationships.

The glamour of Los Angeles had been replaced by rural roads, borrowed rooms, construction sites, and houses where methamphetamine shaped the rhythm of the day. This was not one dramatic fall. It was a relocation of the same search.

Lauren still wanted belonging. She still wanted protection.

She still wanted to escape discomfort quickly. The people offering those things had become more dangerous.

Raul Ambriz Guillen entered this world through his own instability. He had moved from place to place and was looking for work. Accounts differ on the precise sequence through which he became connected to Shane and JP, but the relationship appears to have developed through incarceration, construction work, drugs, or some combination of the three.

Raul needed income. JP had work.

JP also had drugs. When employer and supplier are the same person, dependence becomes harder to escape.

A paycheck can feed the debt. The debt can keep the worker close.

Leaving can become dangerous. Raul was not a spotless victim.

That fact should not be hidden. He had his own history with drugs, poor decisions, and unstable relationships.

None of it made his life disposable. Murder victims are often cleaned up after death so the public can understand their innocence. When they are not easily idealized, attention shifts toward whether they somehow caused what happened.

That's another false choice. Raul could be flawed and still undeserving of execution.

He could owe money and still possess the right to live. He could recognize danger too late and still be a victim of those who chose to kill him.

The relationship between Raul and the group grew complicated. He worked around JP.

He used drugs. He interacted with Shane and Lauren.

At some point, Lauren and Raul became intimate during a party. That encounter would later take on deadly importance.

For Lauren, it may have been one more impulsive decision inside a life where boundaries had grown unstable. For Shane, it became betrayal.

Jealousy in a controlling relationship is not merely an emotion. It becomes evidence of ownership.

Shane didn't need to view Lauren's choices as her own. He could view Raul as someone who had trespassed on property he believed belonged to him.

That possessiveness merged with the debt Raul owed JP. One motive reinforced the other.

JP wanted payment or punishment. Shane wanted revenge.

Raul stood at the intersection. Lauren remained connected to all of them.

The group's relationships were built from unstable materials. Drugs.

Money. Fear.

Sex. Loyalty.

Debt. Each person needed something from another.

No one trusted fully. This kind of social world can feel close because the people spend so much time together. They share substances, secrets, vehicles, and places to sleep.

The intimacy is real. So is the danger.

Relationships inside criminal networks are often conditional. A friend can turn into a threat when he owes money.

A girlfriend can draw suspicion simply by speaking to another man. An employee can become disposable once his debt exceeds his usefulness.

Anyone who knows too much poses a problem. Raul eventually understood that he was in danger.

According to his daughter, he contacted his former wife and said he was with people he believed were dangerous. He needed money. He wanted to get away.

The request came at a moment when the person receiving it could not respond as he hoped. That small failure would later become unbearable in memory.

Families of murder victims often live inside the last missed opportunity. The call not returned quickly enough.

The warning taken less seriously than it should have been. The money not sent.

The invitation not extended. It is natural to search for the moment when the ending might have changed.

The responsibility, however, belongs to those who chose violence. Raul's family didn't kill him because they failed to rescue him in time.

Lauren's childhood didn't kill him. The adult industry didn't kill him. Addiction didn't pull the trigger by itself. People made the decisions. Still, the missed opportunities surrounding all of them remain difficult to ignore.

Treatment after her return, meaningful rehabilitation after an arrest, or family support strong enough to help without enabling her might have changed Lauren's direction. Earlier intervention against Shane or JP might have narrowed the danger around Raul. Enough money to leave could have changed his final days.

Every question reveals a point where the final outcome was not yet fixed. That matters because stories like this are often told as though the murder existed inside Lauren from the beginning.

It did not. The child in her grandmother's house was not destined for prison.

The performer in Los Angeles was not destined to lure a man to his death. The woman returning to Dothan still had choices.

So did the people around her. By the time Raul entered danger, Lauren's options were narrower than they had once been, but they had not disappeared.

She could have left Shane. She could have warned Raul.

She could have contacted law enforcement. She could have removed herself from JP's circle.

Fear, addiction, and dependence made those actions harder. They did not make them impossible.

This is where empathy must remain honest. To understand Lauren's vulnerability is not to erase her responsibility.

She was not merely carried downstream by stronger people. She also moved with them.

She benefited from some of the relationships. She remained when warning signs appeared.

She participated in the world they built. Her dependence on Shane may have been real.

So was the danger she helped create for others by staying close to him. The phrase "predator's dream" returns here with a darker meaning.

A predator may seek someone easy to control. Once controlled, that person can become useful.

She can make calls. Offer reassurance.

Invite someone over. Provide the familiar face that lowers another person's guard.

Aubrey's warmth had once made coworkers want to protect her. The same warmth could make Raul trust her.

The qualities that increased her vulnerability could be turned outward as tools. That possibility is one of the quiet horrors of coercive relationships. The controlled person may become part of the controlling system.

Victimhood and participation can occupy the same body. The road from the airport to Dothan had once looked like a return to failure.

By 2020, Lauren was moving along different rural roads, deeper into a world where failure was no longer the greatest threat. Violence was.

Raul's debt grew more serious. Shane's jealousy hardened.

JP wanted the problem resolved. The language used in criminal circles is often deliberately vague.

Take care of him. Handle it.

Fix the situation. Words soften the act before it occurs.

They allow everyone involved to pretend the meaning remains uncertain. Later, each person can claim to have misunderstood.

But the people inside the conversation usually know. Lauren knew Shane was dangerous.

She knew JP's world was dangerous. Raul knew enough to ask for help getting away.

All of them stood near the final boundary. One person could still refuse.

One warning could still be delivered. One departure could still break the chain.

Instead, the plan moved forward. The Fourth of July approached.

Fireworks appeared in stores and roadside stands. Families prepared cookouts.

Children waited for darkness. In another context, the holiday might have offered Lauren a memory of summer, noise, and brief celebration.

For the people around JP, the explosions offered cover. A gunshot could disappear inside them.

The idea was cold in its practicality. Invite Raul over.

Make the gathering feel ordinary. Wait for the sky to become loud.

Lauren had spent her life searching for a place where she belonged. She had finally found one among people who were preparing to kill a man.

The tragedy was no longer approaching from a distance. It had entered the room.

And this time, Lauren would not simply be caught inside another person's plan. She would help open the door.

The Lure and the Crime

The first firework broke open above the trees in a burst of white light. For a second, the yard flashed bright enough to reveal every face.

Then darkness returned. The smoke drifted low across the ground, carrying the sharp smell of sulfur through the humid Florida night. Another explosion followed from somewhere beyond the property. Then another. The Fourth of July had turned the sky into noise.

Raul Ambriz Guillen stood near the house with people he believed he knew. Lauren was there.

Shane Parker was there. Jeremie "JP" Peters was nearby.

The gathering looked ordinary enough to lower a man's guard. There were fireworks, drugs, conversation, and the loose disorder of a rural holiday party. Nothing about the scene announced that Raul had been brought there to die.

That was the purpose of the invitation. The plan depended on familiarity.

Raul might have hesitated if Shane had called him. He might have questioned an invitation from JP.

Lauren was different. She offered the appearance of safety.

According to the state's case, Lauren helped lure Raul to the property under the pretense of a Fourth of July celebration. He arrived not knowing that a debt, Shane's jealousy, and JP's desire to have him "taken care of" had converged into a plan for murder.

The fireworks were not merely decoration. They were cover.

A gunshot could disappear inside the explosions. That detail reveals the planning more clearly than almost anything else. This was not a sudden argument that spiraled out of control. It was not a frightened reaction or a single impulsive act.

Someone had considered the noise. Someone had considered timing.

Someone had considered how to make a killing sound ordinary. The celebration became camouflage.

Raul reportedly set off fireworks with Lauren. That image is among the most disturbing in the case.

He was participating in the noise intended to conceal his own death. Perhaps he believed the danger he had warned his family about had eased. Perhaps he thought the invitation meant he had been accepted back into the group. Perhaps the drugs softened whatever suspicion remained.

We can't know what he felt in those final minutes. Court testimony and police interviews preserve actions.

They do not preserve the private thoughts of the dead. What remains is the sequence.

Raul was at the house. The fireworks began.

Shane approached. Raul was shot in the back of the head.

Lauren later told investigators that she didn't want to see the shooting and ran around the corner. She said she returned because she feared Shane would hurt her as he had hurt Raul.

Her statement is brief. Its simplicity does not make it clear. Did she know exactly when the shot would come? Did she understand the full plan before Raul arrived? Was she frightened in that moment, or only afterward? Did she believe the threat was real but distant until the weapon fired?

These questions remained beneath the legal facts. One thing is beyond dispute.

Lauren helped bring Raul to the place where he was killed. She knew she was surrounded by dangerous people.

She knew Shane was capable of violence. She remained present when the plan moved toward its final act.

The bullet didn't end Raul's life cleanly. Lauren later described hearing what sounded like snoring. The sound was likely agonal breathing, the involuntary effort of a dying body whose brain could no longer sustain ordinary life.

To someone unfamiliar with severe trauma, it might have sounded as though Raul remained alive in some recoverable sense. He wasn't sleeping. He was dying.

That sound matters because it destroys the distance created by phrases such as "shot in the head" or "executed." Those words can become clinical.

The body was not clinical. It struggled.

Raul made noise. The people around him heard it.

According to testimony, Shane responded with further violence. He shoved dirt into Raul's mouth and nose and struck or dragged him with a shovel as he moved the body toward the wooded area.

The actions suggest panic, cruelty, or both. A plan can feel abstract until the victim refuses to become still. Then the killer confronts the physical reality of what he has done.

The body breathes. It bleeds.

It has weight. It does not cooperate with the neat version imagined beforehand. The violence after the shot may reveal an attempt to force the scene into silence.

Lauren witnessed at least part of that aftermath. Her later account portrayed her as terrified of Shane.

That fear is plausible. She had just watched him shoot a man in the head.

She knew his reputation. She knew his relationship with JP.

She understood that the people around her had already crossed a boundary from which they could not return. Fear after witnessing murder requires no imagination.

The harder question is what fear means for the actions that came before it. Fear and participation can exist in the same moment.

She can understand danger only after helping create it. She can move from complicity to terror in the same night.

The law separates these moments into categories. Human experience does not.

Lauren later said she believed Shane might kill her too. If that fear began after the shot, it may explain why she remained quiet.

It does not explain why Raul was invited. If the fear existed beforehand, it raises another question.

Why did she not warn him? The answer may include addiction, dependence, coercion, loyalty, poor judgment, or self-preservation.

None offers comfort. The tragedy contains no interpretation that makes the decision harmless.

Raul was dead or dying. Lauren didn't call for help.

She didn't report the shooting. She stayed with Shane.

The next part of the story is difficult to understand because it appears so ordinary. Lauren and Shane went to sleep.

The detail has followed me through the entire time I've worked on this book. A man had been shot. His body remained on the property. The sounds of fireworks continued across the countryside. And the two people closest to the killing lay down together.

What allows someone to sleep after participating in murder? Shock might. Drugs might. Exhaustion might. Dissociation might. Moral indifference might. The answer could contain pieces of all of them. Sleep does not necessarily prove calm.

The body can shut down after terror. But going to bed also reflects the terrible human ability to place one reality beside another and continue functioning. The mind compartmentalizes what it can't integrate.

Lauren had practiced compartmentalization for years. Lauren and Aubrey. Private self and public persona. Consent and pressure. Fear and performance. The difference now was that the thing placed outside awareness was a man's death.

Morning didn't make the crime less real. It made concealment necessary.

According to the case record, Shane and JP wrapped Raul's body in black plastic or a tarp. They moved him and buried him in a shallow grave approximately three feet deep.

The grave was not far enough away to erase the act. It only delayed discovery.

The earth became part of the deception. Pine needles, weeds, heat, and rain settled over the place where Raul had been left. For a month, his family didn't know where he was.

That uncertainty is its own form of suffering. A missing person exists in an unbearable space between hope and dread. The family can't grieve fully because confirmation has not arrived. Every unknown number can feel like a call. Every delay allows the imagination to invent another possibility.

Maybe he left. Maybe he's hiding.

Maybe he's in jail. Maybe he's alive.

Those possibilities ended on August 25, 2020, when authorities recovered Raul's remains. The location of the body became known after JP tried to involve Joseph Bailes, a longtime associate, in moving or concealing it further.

Joseph had lived around JP's criminal activity for years. He had benefited from proximity while maintaining that he was not part of the drug business.

The murder forced a boundary. He contacted law enforcement.

This decision does not make him a hero in every part of the story. It makes him the person who finally refused the next step.

Human beings are rarely consistent across every moral question. Someone may tolerate drug dealing, intimidation, and theft, then refuse to help move a body.

The line may be late. It still matters.

Joseph led authorities to the burial site. The grave gave physical form to what had previously been rumor, fear, and conflicting stories.

A body changes an investigation. The missing person becomes a homicide victim.

The people surrounding him become suspects. The questions narrow. Who invited him? Who was present? Who held the gun? Who buried him? Who stayed silent? Lauren eventually spoke.

Her statements became crucial to the prosecution. She identified Shane as the shooter. She described the location, the aftermath, and the concealment. She portrayed herself as someone who participated because she feared him.

Her cooperation helped the state build cases against the others. This created an uncomfortable dual role.

Lauren was both a defendant and a witness. She was implicated in the crime and useful to the prosecution. The justice system often depends on this contradiction.

One participant receives a reduced sentence in exchange for helping convict another. The arrangement can reveal truth.

It can also reward the person whose story best serves the state. That does not mean Lauren lied.

It means her testimony existed inside strong incentives. Every statement should be understood with both facts in view.

She had information only an insider could provide. She also had a reason to minimize her own responsibility.

William Shane Parker was charged with Raul's murder. Jeremie Peters faced charges connected to the killing, concealment, and witness tampering.

Lauren faced the consequences of her own role. The case became more complicated when Shane made statements suggesting that his confession had been shaped in part to protect her.

He said, in essence, that he could handle prison and Lauren could not. He also indicated that he had used information from Lauren and JP when giving his account.

The wording introduced a question that the official narrative never fully resolved. Was Shane confessing because he had committed the shooting?

Was he taking responsibility to shield Lauren? Was he attempting to create doubt after the evidence turned against him?

Was the statement an act of love, manipulation, strategy, or some combination? Only the people present knew exactly what happened at the instant

Raul was shot. The state concluded that Shane pulled the trigger.

Lauren testified that he did. The jury convicted him.

The legal outcome established responsibility. It didn't erase every ambiguity.

True crime audiences often become fascinated by the question of who physically fired the gun. Legally, the question is crucial.

It matters historically. It matters to the people involved.

But it can also become a way of shrinking moral responsibility to a single finger and a single second. Raul didn't die only because someone pulled a trigger.

He died because a group of people created the conditions around that trigger. JP allegedly wanted him punished over a debt.

Shane carried jealousy and a willingness to use violence. Lauren brought Raul into the setting where the plan could succeed.

The body was concealed. The crime remained unreported.

Each act formed part of the chain. Even if another person held the weapon, Lauren's role didn't disappear. If Shane's statement suggested she had been more directly involved, the possibility deepens the uncertainty.

If he was only attempting to protect her, it reveals the strange loyalty binding them even after the murder. Either interpretation leaves the central fact unchanged.

Raul was betrayed by people he knew. Lauren eventually entered a plea of no contest to being an accessory after the fact to second-degree murder with a firearm.

She received a ten-year prison sentence. Her time already served was credited toward the term. Under Florida law, she would be required to serve 85% of that sentence before becoming eligible for release.

Shane received life in prison without the possibility of parole. JP received twenty years.

The sentences established legal distinctions among their roles. Shane would die in custody unless the conviction or sentence changed.

JP would lose decades. Lauren would lose much of her twenties but retain the possibility of returning to society. That difference became part of the public debate.

Some believed ten years was too little for helping lure Raul to his death. Others viewed her as a frightened, addicted young woman controlled by a violent boyfriend.

The disagreement reflects a larger conflict in how we understand accountability. Is punishment measured by the final act?

By intent? By fear?

By cooperation? By the person's capacity for rehabilitation?

The criminal justice system attempts to convert these questions into years. Ten.

Twenty. Life.

The numbers suggest precision. They do not provide moral certainty.

A ten-year sentence can't restore Raul's life. A life sentence can't return him to his daughter.

Prison can remove dangerous people from society and express public condemnation. It can create time for reflection or treatment.

It can also harden trauma, deepen isolation, and return people to society with fewer options than before. Which version would Lauren experience?

Would confinement force her to confront what she had done? Would she receive meaningful addiction treatment?

Would prison teach responsibility or only survival? The answers would not be visible at sentencing.

Courts judge the past. Rehabilitation belongs to a future no judge can guarantee. The courtroom reduced the events into charges, elements, testimony, and sentencing ranges.

Raul's family lived with a different reality. They didn't experience his death as a legal theory.

They experienced his absence. A voice no longer answering.

A birthday passing without him. Questions about his final moments.

The knowledge that he had called for help before disappearing. His daughter described a man who was flawed but loved.

That description deserves space because victims are often simplified too. Raul had made mistakes.

He had used drugs. He had become involved with dangerous people.

He owed money. None of those facts made his life less human. The people who killed him didn't possess moral authority over whether he deserved another day.

Debt is not a death sentence. Addiction is not permission for execution.

Poor judgment does not erase the right to live. The sensational focus on Aubrey threatened to push Raul to the edge of his own story.

Her former career gave the media a marketable angle. Porn star murder plot.

Adult actress lures man to death. The words turned her past into the explanation and Raul's death into the event proving it.

But pornography didn't explain the killing. The immediate forces were closer and uglier. Methamphetamine. Debt. Jealousy. Control. Violence. Fear.

Lauren's career history shaped her vulnerabilities and public image. It didn't create the murder plan.

The distinction matters because false explanations prevent us from recognizing real danger. The threat was not that a former adult performer returned home.

The threat was that an addicted, unstable woman entered a relationship with a violent man inside a criminal drug network and helped him betray someone already trying to escape. That pattern can occur in any community.

It does not require a film set. After sentencing, Lauren entered the Florida prison system. The stage name Aubrey Gold remained online while the state identified her by her legal name and inmate number.

Her scenes continued circulating. People continued watching the version of her recorded before the murder.

The image remained young. The person grew older behind concrete and razor wire.

This is another strange divide in her life. Aubrey Gold never aged.

Lauren Wambles did. The public persona remained fixed in the brief period when she was marketable, while the private woman lived through arrest, court, confinement, and the consequences of a crime no edit could remove.

I have tried to understand what she thought during those first nights in prison. Did she replay the fireworks?

Did she hear Raul's breathing? Did she blame Shane?

JP? The drugs?

Herself? Did she feel relief that she had not received life?

Did that relief create guilt? Did she believe the sentence was fair?

Remorse is difficult to measure from outside. People perform it in court.

They hide it in private. Some feel guilt but avoid responsibility.

Some accept responsibility without displaying emotion in ways others recognize. The absence of visible grief does not always mean the absence of conscience.

It also can't be assumed to prove one. Lauren's own voice remains incomplete.

Her statements to police were shaped by immediate danger and legal consequences. Her testimony served the prosecution. She has not offered a full public account capable of resolving every question.

Perhaps no account could. Memory changes under trauma and substance use.

Self-preservation changes it further. A person may repeat a version so often that the boundary between recall and narrative disappears.

This is why certainty remains dangerous. The official record tells us what the courts accepted. It does not give us access to every private motive.

The case leaves one unresolved question in the center. Who fired the shot?

The state answered Shane. Lauren answered Shane.

The conviction answered Shane. His later words introduced doubt without proving an alternative. That doubt should not be inflated into certainty that Lauren was the shooter.

Nor should it be ignored simply because the legal case reached a conclusion. Responsible skepticism requires remaining inside the limits of the evidence.

We can say that Shane was convicted of killing Raul. We can say that Lauren testified against him.

We can say that Shane later suggested he had taken blame partly to protect her. We can't claim to know more than the people present.

The ambiguity may never be resolved. Moral responsibility is clearer.

Lauren helped lure Raul. She remained silent.

She participated in the aftermath. She eventually cooperated with law enforcement. These actions contain both guilt and a later attempt to assist justice.

One does not erase the other. The same person can help commit a crime and help solve it. The state rewarded the second act without forgetting the first.

Whether ten years adequately balances them is a question readers will answer differently. I find myself returning to the fireworks.

They burst overhead while Raul stood among people he believed he could trust. The noise was chosen because it would make murder harder to hear.

Yet the plan failed in the end. The earth gave back the body.

A friend gave police the location. Lauren gave testimony.

The gunshot hidden inside celebration became part of a public record. Nothing remained buried except Raul himself.

The legal case ended with sentences. The moral questions did not.

Does Shane's life sentence represent justice or only permanent confinement? Does Lauren's ten-year term create the possibility of rehabilitation, or merely postpone the struggle she will face upon release?

What does society owe a person after she has served her punishment? What does she owe the family of the man whose life she helped end?

Can remorse produce redemption? Can redemption exist without forgiveness?

Raul's family is not required to answer those questions generously. They are not obligated to participate in Lauren's rehabilitation.

Their loss is not a lesson designed for someone else's growth. Still, society must decide what punishment is meant to accomplish.

If Lauren leaves prison unchanged, the sentence will have contained her without repairing anything. If she confronts her addiction, understands her role, and builds a different life, Raul will remain dead.

Rehabilitation can't balance that scale. It can only prevent another life from being added to it. The Fourth of July is a holiday built around freedom.

For Raul, it became the last day of his life. For Shane, Lauren, and JP, it began the chain of events that would end their freedom in different measures.

The irony is obvious. The tragedy is quieter.

A man needed help leaving dangerous people and didn't receive it in time. A young woman who spent her life trying to escape control helped deliver another person into it.

A boyfriend who presented himself as a protector became a killer. A man who built power through debt discovered that a shallow grave could not keep his secrets.

No one emerged from the night unchanged. Raul lost everything. His family lost him.

Shane lost the rest of his life outside prison. JP lost two decades. Lauren lost much of the future she had once believed belonged to Aubrey Gold. Yet unlike Raul, the others remained alive to face consequence, regret, denial, or change.

That difference is the final imbalance. They received years. He received none.

Lauren Wambles is not eligible for parole, as the state of Florida officially abolished parole for most crimes in 1983. Instead of parole, Florida operates under a strict "truth-in-sentencing" law. This means that all inmates must serve a minimum of 85% of their total sentence physically behind bars before they can become eligible for early release. Because she cannot get parole, her release timeline depends entirely on her behavior credits.

If she served the maximum sentence (the full 10 years) she would be imprisoned until October 2031. The earliest release (based on the Florida 85% rule), means she must still complete 8.5 years behind bars. If during that time, she maintains perfect institutional behavior and earns maximum "incentive gain-time," this places her earliest possible release date around April 2030. The moment she is released, her 5 year felony probation period begins.

This is the moment she can go on with her life. That's something that Rual Guillen will never be able to do. He's dead. There are no do-overs for him. And his death, at least in part was because of Lauren Wambles. That's a fact and nothing will ever change that.

As she serves her time behind bars, in the Gadsden Correctional Facility just northwest of Tallahassee, Rual's family mourns his loss. She gets to wake up each day and have breakfast, read a book or do other things. Let's not forget that Rual will never get to do any of those things ever again.

Lauren is accessory to second degree murder with a firearm. Whatever you think about her, please never forget that fact.

Professional and Public Perception

The video began with a calm voice and a clean background. No dramatic music. No flashing headlines. No blurred crime-scene photographs. Just a man speaking with the measured confidence of someone accustomed to explaining complicated behavior to a large audience.

I watched Lauren's case files spread across the desk in front of me from my office late at night. Police reports. Court records. Notes from interviews. Screenshots of articles that had repeated the same errors until repetition made them appear true.

On the computer screen, Dr. Todd L. Grande began analyzing Lauren Wambles. His tone was clinical. His conclusion was not.

He described her as impulsive, irresponsible, reckless, self-centered, and driven by sensation. He suggested she had found excitement in Shane Parker's violence and had embraced the murder plot because it made her feel valued. In his reading, Lauren was not primarily a frightened young woman under the influence of a controlling boyfriend.

She was manipulative. She wanted the danger. She later presented herself as a victim to reduce her punishment. I paused the video.

The room went quiet except for the hum of my computer. I had expected a severe assessment. The known facts demanded one. Lauren had helped lure Raul Guillen into a situation that ended with a bullet in the back of his head. Any psychological interpretation that softened that reality into a story of total helplessness would have been dishonest.

Still, the certainty of Dr. Grande's portrait unsettled me. I knew enough of Lauren's history to recognize recklessness. I had witnessed her instability. I had heard about the drinking, the drugs, the damaged hotel rooms, the private bookings, and the moments when friends felt they could not safely leave her alone.

I also knew the woman coworkers remembered as warm, funny, vulnerable, and easy to love. Could those memories coexist with Dr. Grande's darker assessment?

Of course they could. Charm does not prevent cruelty. Vulnerability does not prevent manipulation. Being harmed does not prevent someone from harming others.

But I wondered whether his interpretation replaced one simplification with another. The media had already reduced Lauren to the former porn star who became involved in murder. Now a psychological analysis risked reducing her to a thrill-seeking manipulator who wanted violence because violence made her feel important.

That version was possible. It was not the only possible version.

Professional commentary carries a special kind of authority. A credentialed speaker can make an interpretation sound like a diagnosis, even when the subject has never been examined directly.

Dr. Grande was clear in his public work that he was offering analysis rather than diagnosing people he had not treated. Yet audiences do not always preserve that distinction.

They hear a professional title. They hear a confident explanation.

The explanation becomes truth. Interpreting criminal behavior from a distance leaves the evaluator with records, public statements, court evidence, and known behavioral patterns, but not the subject herself.

He does not see the subject in a clinical room. He can't test inconsistencies.

He can't ask what she remembers, what she minimizes, or what she fears. He can't observe the difference between rehearsed remorse and genuine confusion.

The analysis may be intelligent and still remain incomplete. Lauren's case invited certainty because uncertainty was uncomfortable.

People wanted to know what kind of woman could help lure a man to his death. They wanted a category.

Victim. Predator. Addict. Manipulator. Abused girlfriend. Failed porn star. Each label explained one part and concealed another.

Dr. Grande's analysis placed Lauren firmly on the side of agency. He viewed her actions as chosen, exciting, and self-serving.

This perspective challenged the narrative of coercion. That challenge was necessary.

Women involved in violent crimes are often described in ways that reduce their responsibility, particularly when they are young, attractive, or partnered with older men. The public finds it easier to imagine them as controlled than calculating.

The image of the dangerous boyfriend and vulnerable girlfriend fits a familiar script. The woman is acted upon.

The man acts. Lauren's story did contain a dangerous, controlling man. It also contained her own choices. She contacted Raul. She helped create the invitation. She remained with Shane. She didn't report the murder. Any serious account must resist turning her into a passive object moved through the crime by men.

I had to ask myself whether my own years of advocacy made me more likely to emphasize her vulnerability. I have spent decades watching performers be blamed for harm done to them. I have seen people assume that choosing adult work means consenting to exploitation, violence, or abuse.

That experience taught me to look for power imbalances others ignore. It may also have made me more inclined to see Lauren through those imbalances.

Advocacy can sharpen vision. It can also create blind spots.

The honest response was not to reject Dr. Grande's assessment because it was harsh. It was to test it against the evidence. Was Lauren impulsive?

Yes. Her life showed repeated examples of acting without considering long-term consequences.

Was she sensation-seeking? Probably. She left home young, pursued a stigmatized career, entered unstable relationships, used drugs, and remained close to dangerous people.

Was she manipulative? Possibly.

She had learned to present different versions of herself in different environments. Adult performance itself required controlled presentation, though that skill alone didn't make her deceptive in ordinary life.

Her statements after the murder clearly served a legal purpose. That didn't automatically make them false.

Was she excited by the murder plot? The evidence was less clear. Lauren may have acted from excitement, fear, loyalty, intoxication, pressure, emotional dependence, or several of them at once.

Dr. Grande interpreted her behavior as willing engagement. Others saw a trauma response. The difference matters.

It also may not be fully knowable. I sought additional perspectives from professionals familiar with addiction, coercive relationships, and partner-involved crime. None had evaluated Lauren personally, which imposed the same limitation from the beginning.

Still, their frameworks helped widen the question. One forensic psychologist explained that methamphetamine use can distort judgment, increase paranoia, heighten emotional reactions, and make a person more suggestible within an intense relationship.

That didn't remove agency. It altered the conditions under which agency operated.

Another specialist described trauma bonding, the powerful attachment that can form when fear, affection, control, and intermittent reassurance become entangled. A person in such a relationship may defend the individual who threatens her. She may interpret possessiveness as devotion.

She may comply before an explicit threat is made because she has learned what refusal will cost. Again, none of this excused Lauren.

It complicated the meaning of willingness. Apparent eagerness can conceal fear.

She can act frightened while calculating an advantage. She can feel both.

Human behavior rarely honors the clean boundaries required by public debate. The central disagreement became one of emphasis.

Dr. Grande emphasized personality and choice. Others emphasized addiction, trauma, and coercive dynamics. The strongest interpretation likely included all of them.

Lauren may have possessed traits that drew her toward danger. Her environment may have intensified those traits.

Shane may have controlled her. She may also have used him for protection, status, and access.

She may have feared him and enjoyed the power attached to him. Contradiction is not evidence that one side is false.

It may be the most accurate description of the relationship. The public discussion rarely allowed for that complexity.

Media outlets had already discovered the easiest version of Lauren's story. A former adult film star was involved in a murder.

The connection became the explanation. Headlines used her stage name because Aubrey Gold attracted more attention than Lauren Wambles. Her adult career was treated as the defining fact of her identity, even though it had lasted only a brief portion of her life.

The message was implied rather than argued. Pornography had led to criminality.

Sexual transgression had foreshadowed moral transgression. The fallen woman had fallen farther.

This narrative carries a long cultural history. Women associated with sex work are frequently treated as warnings. Their later suffering becomes proof that the earlier choice was corrupting.

If they experience addiction, abuse, or poverty, the public points backward toward the work and declares the cause solved. The explanation is emotionally satisfying because it protects the audience from harder questions.

Family instability is complicated. Untreated trauma is complicated.

Addiction treatment is expensive. Coercive relationships are difficult to understand.

Economic marginalization implicates systems. Pornography is easier to blame.

The industry connection also gave producers a visual archive. There were photographs.

Scene titles. Promotional images.

A stage name designed to attract attention. True crime media could place the mugshot beside a polished image of Aubrey and allow the contrast to tell the story.

Beauty and ruin. Fantasy and prison.

Rise and fall. The structure was irresistible.

It was also manipulative. The photographs from her career didn't explain the murder. They only made the story more marketable.

Media accounts repeated an incomplete thirty-two-film count and described royalties that traditional adult performers generally didn't receive. These errors mattered because they supported a clean but false story of success, lost income, and inevitable collapse, while ignoring the precarious finances, addiction, family loss, and limited alternatives already documented in her life.

That phrase did more than stigmatize Lauren. It stigmatized everyone who had worked in the adult industry.

The implication was that her criminal behavior grew naturally from the business. People who knew nothing about performers, production, or industry economics could accept the connection because it confirmed what they already believed.

Adult performers are often treated as morally damaged before any evidence of wrongdoing appears. When one becomes involved in a serious crime, the case is presented as confirmation.

Yet most performers never commit violent crimes. They leave the industry, build businesses, raise children, pursue education, marry, divorce, recover from addiction, or continue working without ever entering a courtroom.

Their lives do not become documentaries because ordinary survival lacks spectacle. Lauren's case was exceptional.

The media treated it as representative. That distinction matters because stigma produces material consequences.

A former performer seeking conventional work may be denied employment. A parent can face custody challenges.

A person reporting assault may not be believed. Banks and online platforms may refuse services.

Housing can become harder to obtain. When public narratives connect sex work with moral collapse, they reinforce the very isolation that makes vulnerable people easier to exploit.

The judgment does not remain on the screen. It follows people home.

The public's treatment of Lauren also raised another question. Would the crime have received the same level of coverage if she had never performed under the name Aubrey Gold?

Raul's murder was brutal. Drug debt, jealousy, and a shallow grave would have made it newsworthy.

But the adult industry connection gave the story national appeal. It provided novelty.

The victim became part of a porn-star murder case. Lauren's former career increased attention while pushing Raul deeper into the background.

His daughter's loss could not compete with the visual power of the former performer's photographs. The media claimed to tell a victim's story while centering the accused woman's sexual history.

True crime repeatedly makes this contradiction visible. It says the victim matters most. Then it sells the perpetrator. Raul was not famous.

He had no stage name. He left behind no polished archive. His life had to be reconstructed through family statements, court records, and the circumstances of his death. Lauren's image was already available in abundance.

The imbalance shaped the story before anyone wrote a script. Dr. Grande's analysis didn't rely on the adult industry as the sole cause of the crime. In that sense, it offered a useful correction to sensational reporting.

He focused on behavior. Impulsivity. Sensation-seeking. Self-interest. Manipulation. His framework restored agency that other narratives risked removing.

But it also appeared to move quickly past the significance of trauma, addiction, and coercive attachment. A severe personality description can become another kind of spectacle.

The audience leaves believing the mystery has been solved because the person has been named. Reckless.

Narcissistic. Antisocial. Manipulative. Labels satisfy the desire for distance.

She did this because she's that kind of person. The conclusion protects us from considering how ordinary vulnerabilities can become dangerous under the wrong conditions.

Lauren's path didn't require her to be uniquely evil from childhood. It required accumulated instability, addiction, poor choices, exploitative relationships, and increasing moral compromise.

That possibility is more unsettling because the ingredients are familiar. Many people seek validation.

Many remain in controlling relationships. Many use substances to escape pain.

Many make decisions they regret. Most do not help commit murder.

The difference may lie in timing, circumstance, personality, available support, and luck. This does not make everyone a potential killer.

It reminds us that criminal outcomes can emerge from recognizable human weaknesses without requiring a monster at the beginning. The public prefers monsters.

Monsters are easier to punish. They require no prevention.

Once a person is defined as fundamentally bad, social failures no longer matter. The lack of treatment, the absence of support, and the repeated exposure to exploitation become irrelevant details.

She was always going to do this. That belief is emotionally convenient.

It is rarely provable. The opposite belief can be equally dangerous.

She was only a victim. Shane made her do everything.

The drugs removed her responsibility. Her childhood explains the rest.

This version protects Lauren by erasing the choices that harmed Raul. It also treats her as incapable of moral agency.

Neither extreme respects the evidence. Lauren was neither a monster nor an innocent bystander. She was damaged, impulsive, sometimes charming, and sometimes manipulative, and she participated in a plan that ended a man's life. Fear and excitement may both have been present; exploitation in her past didn't erase her later exploitation of Raul's trust.

Nor was she innocent. The full portrait is harder to hold because it does not provide a clean emotional response.

We can't simply despise her. We can't simply rescue her.

We have to look at what she did and what had been done to her without pretending one cancels the other. The uncertainty surrounding Shane's confession added another layer.

His statement suggested that he accepted blame partly because he believed Lauren could not handle prison. Some interpreted this as evidence that she may have been the shooter.

Others saw it as a controlling man continuing to manage the narrative around the woman he considered his. The statement didn't resolve the case.

It widened the space for speculation. Media outlets thrive in that space.

A question becomes a teaser. Did the porn star pull the trigger?

Was her boyfriend covering for her? The ambiguity attracts attention because it promises hidden truth. But responsible interpretation must recognize the limit.

Shane was convicted of shooting Raul. Lauren identified him.

No reliable evidence established that she fired the weapon. His later words justified continued questioning, not a new conclusion.

Uncertainty should make us careful. It often makes media bolder.

The more unresolved the fact, the more dramatic the presentation. A shadowed reenactment can imply what a court record can't prove.

A narrator can emphasize a pause, a glance, or a phrase until speculation feels like discovery. Viewers remember the emotional suggestion.

They forget the legal qualification. Lauren's public identity became a construction assembled by competing storytellers.

To some, she was a predator who manipulated the state. To others, she was an abused girlfriend with little meaningful choice.

To the media, she was the porn star linked to murder. To former coworkers, she was the bright girl who became increasingly unstable.

To Raul's family, she was one of the people responsible for bringing him to his death. Each perspective contained truth. None contained all of it. This is the problem with public identity.

Once a person becomes a story in industry blogs, different audiences claim ownership. The individual no longer controls which version survives.

Aubrey Gold had once been the identity Lauren created to escape Dothan. After the murder, the media remade Aubrey into something else.

A warning. A villain. A symbol of industry corruption. A clickable contradiction between beauty and violence.

Lauren herself became almost invisible beneath the interpretations. Her own silence contributed to that disappearance. She didn't offer a full public account capable of challenging the narratives around her.

Perhaps legal advice kept her quiet. Perhaps shame did. Perhaps she believed speaking would only make things worse. Perhaps she preferred the ambiguity.

Without her voice, others filled the space. I did too.

Writing this book required me to make choices about emphasis, motive, and meaning. I could not pretend I stood outside the process.

I knew the industry. I had tried to help her.

I had reasons to challenge accounts that blamed the adult industry for everything. That position gave me insight.

It also gave me an argument. The ethical question was whether I could tell Lauren's story without turning her into evidence for my own beliefs.

I wanted to show the media had misunderstood the industry. That was true. I wanted to expose predatory agents and weak regulation. Those failures were real. I wanted readers to understand how financial pressure, addiction, and stigma reduced her options. They did.

But none of those truths could become a defense against Raul's death. The book had to resist using context as a hiding place.

The most honest narrative would leave readers uncomfortable with everyone's certainty, including mine. I do not know exactly what Lauren felt on the night Raul died.

I do not know whether fear outweighed excitement. I do not know whether Shane's control was stronger than her loyalty to him.

I do not know how much of her police statement was memory and how much was strategy. I know what she did.

I know what the courts concluded. I know the patterns that preceded the crime.

Beyond that, interpretation begins. Dr. Grande's analysis deserves consideration because it challenges the instinct to romanticize vulnerability.

His portrait asks us to recognize Lauren's capacity for manipulation, self-interest, and thrill-seeking.

The trauma-based perspective deserves equal consideration because it explains how addiction and coercive attachment can compromise judgment without erasing it. Together, these views offer a more useful question. Not whether Lauren was a victim or a perpetrator.

She was both in different contexts. The question is how victimization, personality, addiction, and agency combined inside the same person until she became capable of participating in irreversible harm.

That's harder than assigning a label. It is also closer to the truth.

Public judgment tends to arrive after the fact. Once the murder occurred, every earlier event was interpreted as a warning.

Her career became evidence of recklessness. Her drinking became evidence of moral decay.

Her relationships became evidence that she sought danger. Her beauty became evidence that she manipulated people.

A life viewed backward can look inevitable. Living forward, it never does.

The young woman laughing with Kendra Cole on her nineteenth birthday didn't know that future commentators would study her behavior for signs of murder. The friends trying to coax her out of a closet didn't know they were witnessing a scene that would later fit a downfall narrative. I didn't know that helping her understand an agency contract would become part of a book about a homicide.

We saw fragments. The ending gave the fragments a shape.

That shape can be mistaken for destiny. The danger in sensational storytelling is not merely that it insults the subject.

It teaches us to wait for catastrophe before we recognize vulnerability. We become skilled at explaining the past and poor at preventing the future.

After Lauren's arrest, everyone could identify the warning signs. The addiction.

The controlling boyfriend. The criminal associates.

The earlier exploitation. The financial collapse.

Where was that certainty when intervention might still have mattered? The question is not an excuse. It is a challenge.

If we believe people like Lauren are dangerous only after they commit irreversible harm, then our systems are designed for punishment rather than prevention. If we identify every vulnerable person as a future criminal, we create another form of injustice. The difficult work lies between those extremes.

Support without naivety. Accountability without dehumanization. Skepticism without spectacle. The public wanted a simple explanation for Aubrey Gold.

The adult industry corrupted her. Shane controlled her. Drugs destroyed her. She manipulated everyone. She wanted excitement. Each statement may contain part of the answer.

None is enough. Raul died because several forces converged and several people chose not to stop what they knew was coming.

Lauren's past shaped her. It didn't command her. Shane influenced her. He didn't erase her will. Addiction impaired her. It didn't remove the difference between right and wrong. The media distorted her story. That distortion didn't make her innocent. The truth remains crowded with contradictions. That may be why it is so often replaced.

A neat story allows the viewer to finish the documentary, close the article, and believe the case has been understood. A complex story follows the viewer home.

It asks what kind of justice is possible when a person is both harmed and harmful. It asks whether rehabilitation can coexist with condemnation.

It asks why society consumes adult performers while refusing to see them as complete human beings. It asks whether Lauren's beauty made people underestimate her guilt or exaggerate her manipulation.

It asks whether the criminal justice system measured her responsibility accurately or merely accepted the testimony it needed. It asks whether prison will change her.

Most of all, it asks us to remember Raul while everyone argues about Aubrey. His death was not a psychological puzzle designed for public entertainment.

It was a life ended. Any interpretation that forgets that has failed before it begins.

Lauren Wambles became many things in the public imagination. Aubrey Gold. Failed star. Addict. Accomplice. Victim. Manipulator. Prisoner.

None of these names tells the whole story. Perhaps the closest we can come to truth is to resist choosing only one. She was the young woman I tried to help. She was the woman who helped lure Raul to his death.

She deserved neither the falsehoods told about her career nor freedom from the consequences of her actions. Holding both truths does not weaken judgment. It makes judgment more honest.

What We Owe the Living

The envelope came back unopened. My name remained in the upper left corner. Lauren's legal name and inmate number were printed across the center in careful block letters. A correctional facility stamp marked the front, along with the bureaucratic language explaining that the letter had not reached her.

I held it for a long time. Inside were questions I had no right to expect her to answer. Did she remember our conversations about her agency contract?

Did she understand how close she had once come to leaving the people controlling her? Did she think about Raul when fireworks sounded outside the prison walls? Did she accept responsibility for bringing him to the place where he died? Was she sober? Was she changing?

The envelope offered nothing back. Lauren remained somewhere behind concrete, locked doors, counts, schedules, and rules. Her days were now measured by the state. Wake-up calls. Meals. Work assignments. Inspections. Recreation periods. Lights out.

The girl who had once fled Alabama because she believed freedom waited elsewhere was living inside a system designed to remove nearly every choice. Aubrey Gold still existed online. Lauren Wambles existed in prison. The distance between those identities had never been greater.

I have never visited her there. My attempts to contact her have gone unanswered. Perhaps she does not want to speak with me. Perhaps my letters never reached her hands. Perhaps she has decided that telling her story would expose wounds she is not prepared to revisit.

Silence can mean many things. It can be shame. Fear. Legal caution. Indifference.

A refusal to allow another person to interpret her life. I can't claim to know which meaning belongs to Lauren.

That limitation matters. This book has followed her from a troubled childhood in Dothan to Las Vegas, Los Angeles, addiction, exploitation, arrest, and murder. It has examined contracts, testing, scene rates, agents, private bookings, coercive relationships, drug networks, court testimony, and media distortion.

Yet the person at its center has not told me how she understands her own life. That absence should make every conclusion more careful. It shouldn't prevent one.

Raul Ambriz Guillen is dead. Lauren helped bring him to the place where he was killed. Shane

Parker was convicted of shooting him. Jeremie Peters helped create the circumstances surrounding the murder and concealment.

The men received long sentences. Lauren received ten years. Those are the legal conclusions.

The larger questions remain unsettled. What could have prevented the crime? What should accountability accomplish? What happens when a vulnerable person becomes dangerous to someone else?

How much responsibility belongs to the individual, and how much belongs to the systems that repeatedly failed to intervene? These questions do not offer the emotional relief of a verdict.

A verdict tells us who must be punished. It does not tell us how to prevent the next funeral. Lauren's life can be read as a series of personal failures.

- She left school.
- She rejected family guidance.
- She entered an industry she didn't fully understand.
- She drank excessively.
- She used drugs.
- She accepted dangerous bookings.
- She stayed with a violent man.
- She participated in criminal activity.

- She helped lure Raul.

Each statement is true or substantially supported by the record. Placed alone, they create the portrait of a person who repeatedly chose destruction.

But another list can be written. She was born to parents who were barely more than children themselves. Her father was largely absent. She moved between unstable family relationships. She entered the adult industry at eighteen with little preparation.

She encountered questionable agents and predatory operators. She worked in a system that paid once while her image could be sold indefinitely. She struggled with addiction without sustained treatment. She left the industry without a meaningful transition plan. She returned to a community where stigma and limited opportunity narrowed her options. She entered a coercive relationship inside a drug-centered criminal world.

These statements are also true. The first list emphasizes responsibility and the second vulnerability. Neither is complete alone. Focusing only on personal failure turns preventable tragedy into a morality play; focusing only on social failure erases Lauren's agency. She was shaped by forces beyond her control and still made choices within them, including one that helped end Raul's life.

Understanding the difference is essential. Compassion can't require pretending Raul's death was an accident of circumstance. Accountability can't require pretending Lauren was born irredeemable.

The two ideas must remain together, even when holding them becomes uncomfortable. Raul deserves more than a brief return at the end of Lauren's story.

His life can't be reduced to the event that revealed her collapse. He was a father. He was loved. He made mistakes. He used drugs and became involved with dangerous people. He reportedly recognized the danger before his death and reached toward family for help.

The help didn't arrive in time. That failure belongs most heavily to the people who killed him, not to the relatives who could not rescue him from a situation they didn't fully understand.

Families often punish themselves after murder. They replay the last phone call. The request for money.

The warning that sounded serious but not yet final. They imagine one different decision creating a different ending.

Perhaps Raul would have left if the money had been available. Perhaps he would have returned to

the same circle days later. Perhaps Shane and JP
would have found him anyway. No one can know.

What we do know is that Raul didn't deserve to
be executed over debt, jealousy, or loyalty inside a
drug operation. His flaws didn't reduce the value of
his life. His family is not required to forgive Lauren.
They are not required to view her sentence as an
opportunity for redemption.

They are not obligated to participate in any
hopeful interpretation of her future. The work of
rehabilitation belongs to Lauren and the institutions
responsible for preparing her to return to society.

Raul's family has already paid enough. I think
about this whenever the word redemption appears.
Redemption is often treated as a gift granted by the
people harmed. It should not be. A victim's family
may never forgive, and the offender must still
decide whether to change. Remorse that depends
on being forgiven is another form of self-interest.

Real accountability requires accepting that
some damage can't be repaired and some
relationships can't be restored. Lauren can't return
Raul to his daughter.

She can't give back the month his family spent
wondering where he was. She can't erase the grave,
the trial, or the years of grief that followed.

The best future available to her will always
contain that truth. Rehabilitation does not balance

the loss. It reduces the chance of creating another one. That may sound insufficient. It is still necessary. Prison is often presented as the final answer to violent crime. A sentence is imposed, the cell door closes, and society turns away with the comforting belief that justice has been served. But has it?

But confinement is a location, not a transformation. Ten years of confinement can end with the same addiction, anger, fear, and inability to function that entered the prison gate.

She may leave worse. Prisons can offer treatment, education, work, faith programs, and counseling. Access varies. Quality varies. Waiting lists grow. Security priorities override therapeutic needs. People learn quickly that emotional vulnerability can be dangerous in an environment built around control.

Survival becomes the first lesson. Rehabilitation may become secondary and often in the prison system, not an option at all.

What will Lauren learn during her sentence? Will she receive effective substance-use treatment, or merely remain unable to access drugs consistently?

Will she examine her relationship with Shane, or preserve it as a story in which she was only afraid? Will she confront the decision to contact Raul? Will she develop practical skills for life after release? Will anyone help her prepare for employment with a felony record and a permanent adult film history?

Or will the system return her to society with fewer resources, deeper stigma, and a new label added to the old ones? Former adult performer. Convicted felon. Accessory to murder.

Each identity closes doors. Legal freedom can coexist with social imprisonment. The question is not whether Lauren deserves to avoid consequences.

She does not. The question is whether society benefits when punishment makes future stability nearly impossible. If the only paths available after prison lead back toward dependency, criminal relationships, and addiction, then the sentence will have delayed danger rather than reduced it.

This is where public conversations about justice often become dishonest. People say they support rehabilitation, but resist housing, employment, education, and healthcare for those who have served their sentences.

They believe in second chances until the person seeks one in their neighborhood or workplace. We release people while denying the conditions required to remain free.

Then we treat failure as proof that they never deserved release. Lauren's future will depend on her choices.

It will also depend on whether choices actually exist. A job offer is a choice. A waiting list is not. Affordable treatment is a choice. A pamphlet handed out before release is not. Stable housing is a choice. A return to the same people and places that fueled addiction is not much of one. The criminal justice system can't create remorse.

It can create conditions where remorse becomes useful. It can provide treatment, education, accountability, and preparation. Or it can warehouse people until the calendar says their punishment is complete. Which purpose are we willing to fund?

Prevention rarely offers the dramatic satisfaction of punishment. There is no courtroom climax when a person enters treatment before committing a violent crime.

No headline announces that financial education prevented exploitation. No documentary follows the performer who read her contract, saved her money, left the industry on her own terms, and built a quiet life.

Success disappears into normality. Failure supplies the content. Aubrey's story received attention because it ended badly enough to be sold. That should disturb us.

It should also direct us toward the less visible lives still capable of different endings. During my years working in the adult industry and as a performer advocate, I've met young people standing at many of the same crossroads Lauren once faced.

They arrived with ambition and little knowledge. Some wanted money. Some wanted attention. Some wanted sexual freedom. Some were escaping families, poverty, abusive relationships, or towns where they felt suffocated. Most believed they understood more than they did.

That's not unique to the adult industry. It's part of being young.

What makes the industry different is the speed and permanence of the consequences. A newcomer can sign a contract she does not understand, film content that will likely remain online for life, and lose control of her public identity before she has learned how to manage a checking account.

The law may consider her fully prepared because she's eighteen. The marketplace may value her because she's not. Age verification proves legal eligibility. It does not prove readiness.

Meaningful reform must begin before the first camera turns on. New performers need plain-language education about contracts, compensation, testing, taxes, consent, boundaries, digital permanence, and career transitions.

They need to understand that a scene rate is gross income, not wealth. They need to know what an agent can legally do, what percentage is reasonable, and how to verify licensing.

They need to recognize that a professional-looking document may be meaningless if the person issuing it lacks authority. They need to know that consent can be changed or withdrawn and that agreeing to a category does not grant permission for every act someone places inside it.

They need realistic information about private bookings and the way terms can shift after arrival. They need safety plans. Transportation and viable housing options Emergency contacts. Mental health resources that do not treat their work as the diagnosis. They need financial education before the first large payment, not after the money is gone.

They need help imagining an exit while the career is still beginning. Planning to leave does not mean failure.

It means acknowledging that most performance careers are brief and that a person's life should be longer than her marketability. These protections can't depend only on individual wisdom.

Telling performers to research better allows businesses to avoid responsibility for the environments they create. Agencies should face meaningful licensing and enforcement.

Producers should maintain clear consent procedures and respond seriously to reports of boundary violations. Platforms should provide transparent systems for disputes, impersonation, stolen content, and payment problems.

Industry organizations should make treatment and counseling accessible before crisis becomes public. None of these measures would eliminate exploitation.

They would make it harder to hide. Regulation must also be designed carefully.

Laws presented as protection can increase danger when they push adult workers into isolation, cut off financial services, or remove access to safer online tools. Moral panic is not reform.

A policy that makes the public feel righteous while increasing a worker's vulnerability is not success. The people affected must have a voice in the rules imposed upon them.

Performers understand risks that lawmakers, commentators, and documentary producers often miss. They know which protections help.

They know which restrictions merely create new gatekeepers. They know how quickly a rule written without them can be used against them. This is why I founded the Performer Education Foundation (performer.training). The idea grew from a simple frustration.

Too many people entered the adult industry without information that should have been available before they signed anything, traveled anywhere, or removed a piece of clothing in front of a camera. Education should not be a privilege reserved for those lucky enough to meet a trustworthy veteran.

It should be accessible. Practical. Free from shame. The foundation was created to give aspiring and current performers the knowledge that so many of us had to acquire through costly mistakes. We discuss legal rights and contract language.

We explain testing protocols and workplace expectations. We talk about money, taxes, savings, and the instability of scene-based income. We address boundaries, coercion, and the difference between a legitimate professional opportunity and a situation designed to exploit urgency. We discuss mental health, substance use, and career transition.

We do not tell adults what choices they are permitted to make. We try to make sure those choices are informed. That distinction is central to my work. Protection should not become another word for control.

Adult performers have spent decades being told that other people know what is best for them. Families, lawmakers, religious groups, producers, agents, platforms, and anti-pornography organizations have all claimed authority over their decisions.

Some concerns are sincere. Sincerity does not guarantee wisdom.

A system can harm people while insisting it is saving them. Education respects agency while reducing the advantage held by those who depend on ignorance. A performer who understands a contract can question it. A worker who knows standard rates can recognize underpayment.

A newcomer who has been taught the signs of coercion may leave before the door closes. A person with savings has more power to refuse. A performer with an exit plan is less dependent on the next booking. Information does not prevent every bad decision.

It changes the conditions in which decisions are made. With help from former and current adult performers, business professionals, advocates, and labor organizers, I have provided education and training to many people seeking a clearer understanding of adult work. Over a thousand individuals have taken advantage of the free programs and resources at performer.training.

Each person arrived with different needs. Some wanted to perform. Some wanted to leave. Some had already signed agreements they regretted. Some needed help identifying whether an agent's threats had legal force. Some needed permission to imagine a future beyond the identity the internet knew. The victories were often small enough to remain invisible.

A contract not signed. A fee challenged. A boundary stated clearly. A dangerous booking refused. A portion of income moved into savings. A performer choosing treatment before losing everything. These moments do not create headlines. They may prevent them.

I can't say education would have saved Lauren. She knew people who offered guidance. I offered some of it myself. Knowledge competes with addiction, fear, pride, and emotional dependence. Lauren could understand the danger and still walk toward it.

But better preparation might have altered particular choices. Earlier education might have changed particular decisions: a realistic explanation of the economics, financial counseling, independent contract review, and an easier route away from predatory representation. Affordable therapy, substance treatment, career-transition support, and a return to Alabama that did not mean losing money, work, identity, and hope might also have widened her options.

None of these questions erases the choice she made concerning Raul. They ask whether the circumstances surrounding that choice could have been changed before another person paid the final cost.

The phrase systemic failure can become too broad to mean anything. A system does not pull a trigger.

A system does not make a phone call inviting someone to a party. People act. Yet systems determine which risks are ignored, which harms are normalized, and which forms of help remain inaccessible. The adult industry failed when predatory operators could continue working openly.

The healthcare system failed when addiction and trauma remained untreated. The legal system failed when repeated arrests didn't produce meaningful rehabilitation.

The family system failed in ways both understandable and painful. The economic system failed when a young woman could appear successful while earning too little to build security.

The media failed when it transformed a complicated life into a warning about pornography. Lauren failed Raul.

All of these statements can be true at once. Responsibility is not a pie divided into portions until the individual receives none. Recognizing institutional failure does not reduce personal guilt.

It identifies where future intervention remains possible. We can't change Lauren's decision on July 4, 2020.

We can change whether another eighteen-year-old enters a high-risk industry without preparation. We can change whether addiction treatment requires money and insurance a struggling worker does not possess. We can change whether victims of controlling relationships are forced to choose between danger and homelessness. We can change whether people leaving prison receive actual support.

We can change whether former adult performers are denied ordinary opportunities because the public continues consuming work it refuses to forgive them for creating. Destigmatization is not the same as celebration. A society can recognize adult performers as human beings without endorsing every company, scene, or decision in the industry.

It can condemn exploitation without treating all performers as exploited. It can support those who choose the work and those who regret it. It can recognize that dignity does not depend on sexual history. Stigma is often defended as a deterrent.

People believe shame will discourage entry into the industry. In practice, shame frequently isolates those already inside.

It makes performers less likely to report assault. It gives abusive agents more power because the worker fears family discovery. It makes therapy more difficult when professionals treat the occupation as the cause of every problem. It limits employment options after exit.

It increases dependence on the same industry people are being told to leave. Shame doesn't create safety. It creates silence. The public also needs education.

Sensational portrayals shape policy and prejudice. When documentaries and news programs misunderstand scene rates, royalties, agency practices, or the scale of a performer's work, their errors do more than weaken accuracy.

They create false causes. Aubrey's adult career becomes the reason for her criminality. The audience learns to fear the occupation instead of recognizing the combination of addiction, coercive control, criminal association, and repeated failed intervention.

That misunderstanding directs reform toward the wrong target. Closing a website would not have saved Raul.

Stopping a legal adult from performing would not have treated Lauren's addiction. Moral condemnation would not have taught her to recognize a predatory contract.

The solutions are less dramatic. Education. Healthcare. Financial stability. Enforceable labor protections. Accessible treatment. Domestic violence resources. Reentry support. These measures lack the emotional force of a ban or prison sentence. They may accomplish more.

I don't want Lauren's story used to argue that the adult industry is uniquely destructive. It's not.

Many people work in the adult industry and build stable, healthy, productive lives. Some enjoy the work. Some own companies. Some save money, pursue education, and transition successfully when they choose.

Their experiences deserve recognition because tragedy creates a distorted sample. The people who leave quietly are rarely interviewed.

The performers who maintain boundaries do not become cautionary tales. The businesses that follow ethical practices receive less attention than the operators who abuse trust.

Acknowledging successful experiences does not require ignoring exploitation. Both exist.

An honest reform movement must be able to say that adult work can be chosen and that choice does not eliminate vulnerability. It must protect workers without insisting they are incapable of consent.

It must confront abusive practices without treating the entire workforce as damaged. It must listen to the people doing the work.

The same complexity should guide how we think about Lauren. She is not representative of every adult performer.

Her crime does not reveal the moral character of an industry. She is one person whose vulnerabilities intersected with particular failures and choices until the outcome became catastrophic.

Her story matters because it is specific. It also reveals patterns that extend beyond her. Young people seeking identity through visibility.

Workers entering unstable labor without education. Women mistaking control for protection.

People medicating trauma with substances. Families responding to frightening choices with rejection. Courts processing addiction without treating it.

Prisons being asked to repair damage they were designed mainly to contain. These are not adult industry problems alone.

They are human problems. The adult industry made some of them easier to sensationalize.

I return to the envelope. It sits among my notes as evidence of a conversation that never occurred. Part of me still wants Lauren to explain herself.

I want to know whether she recognizes the people who tried to help her. I want to know whether she believes she was controlled or whether that explanation now feels too convenient. I want to know what she remembers about Raul's breathing after the shot. I want to know whether the unanswered letters represent refusal, shame, or simple prison bureaucracy.

Perhaps I want answers that no person could provide honestly, even if she tried. Memory protects the self. Addiction fragments time. Fear reshapes motive.

Years of repeating a legal narrative can harden it into personal truth. Lauren's account would matter.

It would not become the final word. There may be no final word.

There is only the record, the testimony, the grave, the sentence, and the lives that continued after Raul's ended. Lauren will one day leave prison, possibly as early as April 2030.

When she does, she will face another version of the question that followed her from Dothan to Las Vegas and back again. Who is she now? Aubrey Gold will still be searchable. Lauren Wambles will carry a felony conviction.

Employers will find both. Strangers will believe they know her from scenes recorded when she was barely an adult or from documentaries created after her arrest. She will need to build a private life beneath identities other people own.

Whether she succeeds will depend partly on what she has done during confinement. Has she confronted addiction? Has she accepted responsibility? Has she developed the patience required for ordinary work and ordinary days?

Has she learned to live without the intensity that defined so much of her life? No program can answer these questions for her. But without support, the questions may become impossible to answer well.

Reentry should begin long before release. Treatment should continue after the prison gate opens. Housing should not depend on returning to the relationships that contributed to the crime.

Employment programs must account for digital stigma as well as criminal records. Mental healthcare must address guilt, trauma, addiction, and public notoriety.

These resources are not rewards. They are public safety.

A person leaving prison will live somewhere. She will work somewhere or remain unemployed. She will either build stable relationships or return to unstable ones.

Society can influence those conditions. Refusing to do so does not strengthen accountability. It increases risk. Lauren's future does not belong to me.

It doesn't belong to the adult industry, the media, or the audience that consumed her downfall. It belongs to her, within the limits created by what she has done.

She can't choose whether the past follows her. She can choose what she does when it arrives. I hope she changes. That hope is not forgiveness on Raul's behalf. It is not a claim that ten years erase her role.

It is the belief that no society becomes safer by insisting people remain the worst version of themselves forever. Redemption, if it comes, will not be a dramatic moment. It will be a collection of ordinary decisions. Sobriety on a difficult day. Honesty when a lie would be easier. Work that offers no fame.

Acceptance that some people will never trust her. A refusal to seek protection from violent men. A willingness to hear Raul's name without retreating into excuses. Perhaps service to others. Perhaps silence. Perhaps a life so uneventful that no one writes about it again. That would not undo the past. It might prevent another tragedy.

This book began with a phone lighting a dark room. A former performer had been arrested in connection with murder.

The alert reduced a life to a headline before I had finished reading it. I knew the woman in the photograph, but not as well as I first believed.

I knew the industry she had entered. I knew some of the people who had influenced her. I had tried to help with one contract at one moment. I didn't know where her life was going. None of us did.

That uncertainty is the reason this story should not end with the comforting claim that the signs were obvious. They are always obvious afterward.

The task is to recognize vulnerability before it becomes evidence in a criminal case. To respond before the mugshot. Before the shallow grave. Before a family must learn what happened to someone they loved.

Compassionate prevention is not softness. It requires seeing danger without abandoning the person showing signs of it. It requires boundaries, treatment, education, and accountability before punishment becomes the only remaining tool.

We will never prevent every crime. We can refuse to wait passively for one.

Raul's death should not become merely the conclusion of Lauren's downward spiral. It should remain a demand. Protect people before desperation makes them easier to control. Treat addiction before it reorganizes a life.

Regulate those who profit from inexperience. Give workers knowledge before asking them to sign away rights. Help people leave industries and relationships without requiring them to become destitute first.

Prepare prisoners to return before opening the gate. Tell the truth about victims, even when their lives were complicated.

Tell the truth about offenders, even when the truth contains suffering. The choice is not between empathy and responsibility. We need both. Without empathy, justice becomes revenge. Without responsibility, empathy becomes denial. Raul deserved a society that protected his life.

Lauren deserved a society that intervened before she helped take it. Now she owes the future something in return. She owes it honesty. Change. The refusal to harm again. Whether she will give those things remains unknown.

The unopened envelope can't answer. It rests on my desk beside the records of everything that can no longer be changed. Beyond the window, evening settles. Soon the room will be dark.

Somewhere in Florida, Lauren will hear the final count of the day. A door will close. The state will confirm that she remains where the sentence placed her.

Raul will remain absent. His family will carry another night without him. And outside those walls, other young people will stand at the beginning of choices they do not yet understand.

They are the reason the story must continue. Not as spectacle. As warning. As education. As work.

About The Author

Kelli Roberts is an award-nominated producer, marketing executive, branding strategist, and writer with three decades of experience in the adult industry.

Since beginning her career in 1996, she has worked with leading companies, managed high-profile digital properties, and consulted on marketing and brand development across the industry.

Through years of firsthand experience, Kelli Roberts gained a unique perspective on the culture, personalities, and power structures that shape the adult entertainment world.

Her work has placed her at the intersection of media, celebrity, public perception, and controversy, providing rare insight into stories that often remain hidden from public view.

In *If Looks Could Kill: The Aubrey Gold Story,* Kelli Roberts draws on that experience to examine one of the industry's most controversial criminal cases.

Combining investigative research, court records, and insider knowledge, she explores the complex relationship between beauty, fame, privilege, and justice.

Beyond her professional work, Kelli Roberts has been a vocal advocate for performer rights, industry transparency, and informed public discussion about the adult industry.

Her writing seeks to bridge the gap between sensational headlines and the human realities behind them, bringing nuance and context to stories that are often misunderstood.

Learn more about Kelli Roberts at **kelli.net**.